Dickens, women and language

For Penny Boumelha

Dickens, women and language

Patricia Ingham

HARVESTER
WHEATSHEAF

New York   London   Toronto   Sydney   Tokyo   Singapore

First published 1992 by
Harvester Wheatsheaf
Campus 400, Maylands Avenue
Hemel Hempstead
Hertfordshire, HP2 7EZ
A division of
Simon & Schuster International Group

Typeset in 10/12 pt Baskerville
by Keyboard Services, Luton

Printed and bound in Great Britain by
Billing and Sons Ltd, Worcester

British Library Cataloguing in Publication Data

A catalogue record for this book is available from
the British Library

ISBN 0-7450-1290-6 (hbk)
ISBN 0-7450-1253-1 (pbk)

1 2 3 4 5   96 95 94 93 92

Contents

Note on references

The sources of quotations in the text are indicated by the author's surname and date of publication. Full reference is given in the References at the end of the book.

Quotations from Dickens' works are (with the exception of six novels) from the New Oxford Illustrated Dickens, 21 vols, (1947–58). Where an Oxford Clarendon edition is available it has been used: *Oliver Twist* (Tillotson 1966); *The Mystery of Edwin Drood* (Cardwell 1972); *Dombey and Son* (Horsman 1974); *Little Dorrit* (Sucksmith 1979); *David Copperfield* (Burgis 1981); and *Martin Chuzzlewit* (Cardwell 1982). References to letters are from the *Nonesuch Edition* (Dexter 1938), the *Pilgrim Edition* (House *et al.* 1965–88), and *Letters from Dickens to Angela Burdett-Coutts 1841–65* (Johnson 1952).

Acknowledgement

I should like to express my deep gratitude to Jenny Harrington, without whose expert skills, advice and support this book could not have been written.

Chapter 1

Representation and language

Introduction

The younger lady was in the lovely bloom and spring-time of womanhood; at that age, when, if ever angels be for God's good purposes
enthroned in mortal forms, they may be, without impiety, supposed to
abide in such as hers.

She was not past seventeen. Cast in so slight and exquisite a mould;
so mild and gentle; so pure and beautiful; that earth seemed not her
element, nor its rough creatures her fit companions. The very intelligence that shone in her deep blue eye, and was stamped upon her
noble head, seemed scarcely of her age, or of the world; and yet the
changing expression of sweetness and good humour; the thousand
lights that played about the face, and left no shadow there; above all,
the smile; the cheerful happy smile; were made for Home; for fireside
peace and happiness. (Rose Maylie in *Oliver Twist*, pp. 187–8)

Dickens' depiction of female characters is not usually seen as
contradictory but the critical method employed in what follows
uses such a reading. At the time when he wrote and later
in the nineteenth century there was a predictably sentimental response to 'ideal' figures like Rose Maylie. Some male critics, such
as Samuel Phillips in 1861, praised him for his distillation of young
womanhood into a transcendent 'reality': his women . . . hold an
eminence which women may and do reach in the world, and which
mere purity and love do not suffice to attain (Collins 1971: 263).
But even early readers were not unanimous in their praise. That

1

trenchant female, Margaret Oliphant, took a different perspective in 1865:

> Mr. Dickens is evidently ambitious of achieving a heroine – witness his vehement endeavour to make something of Ruth Pinch, his careful elaboration of Dolly Varden, and even the pains he has taken with Dora . . . but we cannot say that the effort is successful in Esther Summerson. In the ordinary types of heroines – in the Agnes Wickfield, the Ada, the Kate Nickleby – Mr. Dickens is very generally successful. Those young ladies are pretty enough, amicable enough, generous enough to fill their necessary places with great credit and propriety, but to produce an individual woman is another and quite different matter.
> (Collins 1971: 334)

Oliphant sees unreality where Phillips sees reality in its transcendent form; and these become the conventional terms of the binary opposition within which Dickens' heroines are discussed – as real or stereotypical.

It was the latter view which prevailed to become a cliché of literary criticism. A routine classification developed in which the heroines are seen as quite unrelated to other stereotypes like the comic grotesques exemplified by Mrs Gamp in *Martin Chuzzlewit* or Mrs Skewton in *Dombey and Son*. The first innovation in this study therefore will be to reassemble the supposedly splintered representations of females and femininity commonly seen as strewn across the texts in a fairly random fashion. The process of producing a cohesive account will eventually reveal the contradictory fears and desires that underlie Dickens' eccentric account.

Some relatively recent assessments of women in Dickens' texts have lent a spurious unity to their critiques by relating each woman to an archetypal figure in his life. John Carey, for instance, in *The Violent Effigy* (1973), sees Dora Spenlow as a transform of Maria Beadnell; Little Nell, Ruth Pinch, Agnes Wickfield and Little Dorrit as 'partial reflections' of Dickens' sister-in-law, Mary Hogarth's 'purity and blessedness' (Carey 1973: 157–8). He seems to equate Ellen Ternan, 'his young mistress', with Lizzie Hexam in *Our Mutual Friend* (*ibid.*, p. 27). Michael Slater, in his *Dickens and Women* (1983), is even more thorough-going in his use of this approach and bases his account on a first section called 'Experience into art': Dickens' mother is the inspiration for Mrs Nickleby and Mrs Micawber (pp. 16ff.); his sister, Fanny, for Kate Nickleby, Agnes Wickfield, Ruth Pinch and Florence Dombey, while she 'blends' with his memory of Mary Hogarth to form 'the ultimate sisterly ideal in the "Star"' (p. 36), and with his first love, Maria Beadnell, in the Fanny of 'The child's story' (pp. 25ff.); Maria herself is Miss Snevellicci in *Nicholas Nickleby*, Dora Spenlow and Flora Finching (pp. 60ff.); Mary Hogarth turns into Rose Maylie, Kate Nickleby, Little Nell, Mary Graham in *Martin Chuzzlewit* and Agnes Wickfield (pp. 77ff.); Dickens' sister-in-law, Georgina, becomes Esther Summerson in *Bleak House* and possibly Little Dorrit (pp. 163ff.). And so it goes on, with most of the women in his novels explained away as blends of women in his life. Certainly the two interact, but as I hope to show in my final chapter, it is more appropriate to deal with the interaction in terms of life imitating art; of life *as* literary art.

The approach offered here differs radically from Carey's and Slater's. It gives a coherent account of the women in Dickens' novels through an examination of the language in which they are constructed, that common medium for the ideologies of class and gender which inform and evaluate them. This relocates such figures where they belong: in the text, not in some specious hinterland behind it. Each instance of a stereotype can then be shown to be the particular exponent of an abstraction; such images are like examples of a literary genre which never occur in a pure and unmodified form. To write of a work as 'a courtly love lyric' or 'a medieval romance' is to refer to individual modifications of an assumed norm. Similarly, each example of a female stereotype is a variation on it; and its multiple forms turn it into a site for possible linguistic change. This kind of change always starts with an individual whose idiosyncratic variants create flux not stasis. Her/his usage may in time enter the communal system, as has happened with the general acceptance of *gay* to mean 'homosexual'. The mechanism of change is evident here because it is publicly recognised to be the result of a deliberate attempt by a group of individuals to modify the system. Not all overt efforts work so effectively. Feminists devised *spokesperson* as a term for 'mouthpiece (unmarked for gender)'; but the communal language seems to be now accepting it in an adapted sense 'mouthpiece (not male)'. This account of such highly visible but rare shifts and half-shifts is a way of illustrating the invisible process and fluidity always present in language, particularly in culturally contested areas.

The examples above are taken from the fields of gender and sexuality but the same is equally true of the related issue of class, which is also volatile. This is clear in our uneasy contemporary alternation of *lady* meaning 'middle-class female' (*perfect lady*) with *lady* meaning 'female to be respected (unmarked for class)' (*she's a busy lady*). Similarly *woman* is sometimes 'non-middle-class female' (*cleaning woman*) and sometimes 'female (unmarked for class)' (*women only*).

What is true today was also true in the early nineteenth century: issues of gender, sexuality and class were in cultural and linguistic flux. They were also, as Lynda Nead shows in relation to Victorian painting in *Myths of Sexuality*, inextricably linked. She validates amply her claim that 'The representation of woman can never be contained within an investigation of gender; to examine gender is to embark on an historical analysis of power which includes the formation of class and nation' (1988: 8).

What I wish to do, therefore, in this account is to characterise the individual reworking by Dickens of images of women through close scrutiny of his texts. I discard the idea that the language of sexism absolutely speaks the man, and am concerned to distinguish Dickens' own sexist 'idiolect' or personal language, and to analyse its interaction with prevailing codes for the representation of women. In order to do so, his work will be compared with some 'non-fictional' texts of the mid-Victorian period in which such codes can be seen at work in a way that is generally similar and yet, of course, dissimilar. These works in this chapter are mainly the writings of the sociologist, Sarah Stickney Ellis. Such a comparison makes clear that what is going on in both kinds of texts is the representation of women according to existing linguistic conventions; but, in the novelist's case, with a distinctively Dickensian colouring.

Nead's claim about a code encompassing class as well as gender is borne out in relation to language by Ellis' work. For her, nationalism is also omnipresent: her first volume is entitled *The Women of England*, with the adjectival phrase lending a different emphasis from that of the simple adjective. It subordinates gender to nationality rather than the other way round, as the use of the adjective *English* would have done. The same phrase recurs as part of the title of each separate volume: her project is always to describe 'the characteristics of the women of England'. Dickens, on the other hand, merely contains his treatment of gender within a framework of chauvinism that assigns French nationality to his cold-blooded murderer, Hortense, in *Bleak House*, and personifies the worst aspects of the French Revolution in French women generally rather than men:

The men were terrible, in the bloody-minded anger with which they looked from windows, caught up what arms they had, and came pouring down into the streets; but, the women were a sight to chill the boldest . . . from their children, from their aged and their sick . . . they ran out with streaming hair, urging one another, and themselves, to madness with the wildest cries and actions. . . . Give us the blood of Foulon, Give us the head of Foulon, Give us the heart of Foulon, Give us the body and soul of Foulon, Rend Foulon to pieces, and dig him into the ground. . . . With these cries, numbers of women, lashed into blind frenzy, whirled about, striking and tearing at their own friends until they dropped into a passionate swoon. (*A Tale of Two Cities*, pp. 212-13)

The ultimate Terror then is seen to be female but mercifully alien. Its precise focus is Thérèse Defarge, who delights in hewing off the head of the murdered governor of the Bastille (*A Tale of Two Cities*, p. 209).

Such demons, wandering Grendel-like in their outer darkness beyond England, are the infamous 'other', the negative that defines that positive, the true Englishwoman. This polarising is evident in the scene between Thérèse Defarge and Lucie Manette's companion, the genteel Miss Pross, who, covering the latter's escape from Paris, symbolically slays the French Fury:

'I am a Briton,' said Miss Pross, 'I am desperate. I don't care an English Twopence for myself. I know that the longer I keep you here, the greater hope there is for my Ladybird. I'll not leave a handful of that dark hair upon your head, if you lay a finger on me!' (p. 349)

Though nationalism sets limits, however, it is not interwoven into the detail of many of Dickens' images of women as it is into Ellis'; so little more will be said about it.

It is also when Ellis is busy interlocking gender and nationalism that she allows us to see in her 'non-fictional' work the process of representation taking place. Faced with the English women that she knows, she feels obliged to add a qualification to her eulogy:

I ought, perhaps, in strict propriety, to say what *were* their character-istics; because I would justify the obtrusiveness of a work like this by first premising that the women of England are deteriorating in their moral character, and that false notions of refinement are rendering them less influential, less useful, and less happy than they were. (Ellis 1839: 10)

This displaces a perceived gap between actuality and the constructions of women in her text onto a historical axis. Elsewhere she bridges the same gap by a claim that her work is not reflectional but normative:

> In order to speak with precision of the characteristics of any class of people, it is necessary to confine our attention as much as possible to that portion of the class where such characteristics are most prominent; and, avoiding the two extremes where circumstances not peculiar to that class are supposed to operate, to take the middle or intervening portion as a specimen of the whole. (1839: 13)

A similar process of representation occurs in all texts, including Dickens'.

The relation of this kind of construction of gender to the class system is clearly discernible in Ellis' work in a way which confirms Nead's claim that, in the conventional signifying system of the Victorian period, the working classes (the plural is normal) are usually represented as 'other' to the middle classes, just as women are defined in terms of their otherness to men (and Englishwomen in terms of their otherness to non-English women). She argues that they were perceived to constitute 'a term of difference which confirmed the superiority of bourgeois codes of morality and respectability. The working classes were represented as "criminal and dangerous"' (Nead 1988: 76). With working-class women this criminality was linked with sexuality through the supposed location of promiscuity among them. This will be discussed more fully in chapter 3. In general terms femininity was constructed around a moralised account of the maternal (not sexual) instinct which supplied a structuring opposition to competitive, aggressive and sexualised masculinity. Crucial to this opposition was the containment of the virtuous and sexless middle-class woman by the oppositional figure of her defining other, the sexual and outcast fallen woman or prostitute, representative of the working classes.

Ellis, though she presents a more discreet denigration of the working classes, illustrates Nead's point as she moves from Englishness to middle-classness:

> In looking around, then, upon our 'nation of shopkeepers', we readily perceive that by dividing society into three classes, as regards what is commonly called rank, the middle class must include so vast a portion of the intelligence and *moral power* of the country at large, that it may not improperly be designated the pillar of our nation's strength, its base

being the important class of the laborious poor, and its rich and highly ornamental capital, the ancient nobility of the land. (Ellis 1839: 14; my italics)

The 'laborious poor' are elsewhere alluded to in the less flattering way proposed by Nead as conventional:

England as a nation has little to boast of besides her intellectual and her moral power. It is in this that her superiority is felt and acknowledged by the world. . . . That this power is chiefly lodged with the middle classes, I think all have agreed; and that, originating in them, it is made to operate more extensively through the efficient instrumentality of a *comparatively* well-ordered and wisely governed population of working people. (Ellis 1843a: 208-9; my italics)

Much time is spent by Ellis delimiting the middle classes, separating off the others. On the one side are the upper classes: richness and ornament are theirs of right and worn with grace, but they are an unsuitable model for the bourgeoisie, who turn these merits into ostentation and triviality. It is essential that the middle classes avoid showy pretensions to the habits and dress of their superiors. The message is clear: keep out. On the other side are the poor who, if laborious, are worthy, but who become unworthy by encroaching in the shape of servants acting as a fifth column amongst middle-class children:

with the highest esteem for the general character of a truly respectable servant, I still think that the best of them are too much under the influence of false and limited views of things in general, to admit of their being desirable companions for children in their moments of unrestrained confidence. (Ellis 1843b: 247)

The message again is clear: beware. The guardian which will ward off dangers is a crucial concept in this context, that of *taste* in which moral, social and aesthetic standards are fused and confused:

Taste, unquestionably, gives a bias to the character, in its tendency to what is elevated or low, refined or vulgar; but after all, the part of taste is only that of a witness called into a court of justice, to test the value of an article, which has some relation to the great and momentous decision in which the judge, the jury, and the court, are so deeply interested. As taste is that witness, religion is that judge; and it is only as the one is kept subservient to the other, that it can be rendered conducive to our happiness or our good. (Ellis 1845: 176)

In middle-class women this manifests itself as the 'delicacy' involving sexual ignorance that will be discussed in chapter 2.

The morally central position of the middle classes guarded by good taste is found also in Dickens' work. The fact was recognised somewhat ironically by Matthew Arnold, writing in 1881 on *David Copperfield*: 'Intimately, indeed, did Dickens know the middle class; he was bone of its bone and flesh of its flesh. Intimately he knew its bringing up' (in Collins 1971: 267). Arnold, of course, is critical of middle-class philistines, but in Dickens' account of society they are the crucial source of a benevolence which, if in lavish supply, would do away with the need for any more radical reform:

> Oh for a good spirit who would take the house-tops off, with a more potent and benignant hand . . . and show a Christian people what dark shapes issue from amidst their homes, to swell the retinue of the Destroying Angel as he moves forth among them! For only one night's view of the pale phantoms rising from the scenes of our too-long neglect. . . . Bright and blest the morning that should rise on such a night: for men, delayed no more by stumbling-blocks of their own making, which are but specks of dust upon the path between them and eternity, would then apply themselves, like creatures of one common origin, owning one duty to the Father of one family, and tending to one common end, to make the world a better place! (*Dombey and Son*, p. 620)

So from early on in Dickens' work the mitigation of social ills by soup-kitchen benevolence, doled out by the middle classes, appears in the Brownlows, who rescue Oliver Twist from 'the very dregs of life' to feed him on or turn him into its 'froth and cream' (Preface to the third edition, p. xv); in the Cheeryble brothers, who service the Nickleby family; in the Garlands in *The Old Curiosity Shop*; and later in Jarndyce in *Bleak House*. The upper class are mainly absent, aside from the Dedlocks, except in the shape of marginal figures like Hawk and Verisopht in *Nicholas Nickleby* or the effete cousin in *Bleak House*, who serve as warnings to possible middle-class invaders to keep out. And just as Dickens is, like Ellis, preoccupied with the middle section of society, so too his account of gender and class can be seen, like hers, as transposed one into the other.

It is sometimes claimed that in this period such transposition was often an attempt to displace onto gender 'the more politically volatile issue of class so as to address and manage it symbolically' (Poovey 1989: 18). But, failing agreement about this aspect of the general code, it seems preferable to try to decide from Dickens' own novels which is being displaced onto which. An illustration of the difficulty of answering the question is provided by the treatment of Lizzie Hexam in *Our*

Mutual Friend, a novel in which, almost by accident, the narrator confronts the relationship between class and virtue in a woman. She is identified early on as a marriageable heroine when the dissolute barrister Eugene Wrayburn spies on her through the window of her father's hovel, 'a deep rich piece of colour, with the brown flush of her cheek and the shining lustre of her hair' (p. 164). But she is a girl whose father drags corpses from the Thames for a living and is thought to rob them when possible. Consequently, as befits her station and parentage, her speech is coloured by lower-class markers (*a-looking, a'most, in a tremble, in revenge-like, the like of that,* pp. 27ff.). It is also lexically homely: she offers her father meat that is 'hot and comfortable' and 'a drop of brandy' (pp. 74–5). This form of speech becomes an obstacle when Wrayburn, after she has saved his life, turns from thoughts of seduction to intentions of marriage. Society questions whether 'a young man of very fair family, good appearance, and some talent, makes a fool or a wise man of himself in marrying a female waterman, turned factory-girl' (*Our Mutual Friend,* p. 817). Such questionings are satirised, but the fact remains that before Lizzie can marry Wrayburn her speech has to be purged of its lower-class associations; and so it is. She uses no more markers of the kind referred to and acquires a syntactically fluent command of speech. Verbally, it is implied by this alteration, she is now a moral match for Wrayburn since she speaks the only language fit for heroes/heroines in the mid-Victorian novel. Unfortunately, the foregrounding of moral assessments makes a reformed rake seem now an unworthy match for her. This uneasy handling of the convention that articulates social class through linguistic status, which is in turn equated with moral status, reveals the difficulty in reading this text as one which displaces class onto gender or vice versa. Both issues appear equally 'volatile'.

It is not surprising that in the language used by Ellis, Dickens and others, like Geraldine Jewsbury or Florence Nightingale, who write from different viewpoints about women, negatives are as important as positives/affirmatives. Wide and varying use was made of them.

The fact that negation or absence of something ('zero expression' to the linguist) can be meaningful in a positive way is evident from the example of blanks in a railway timetable which signify 'in this specific period there are no trains from this specific station to that'. Ellis provides clear illustrations of the use of negation in the language that she shares with Dickens. It is evident even in her overall plan. She lays out her exposition of the womanly ideal in four volumes: a comprehensive account of *The Women of England, their Social Duties and Domestic Habits* (1839), which is then subdivided into *The Wives of England* (1843a), *The Mothers of England* (1843b), and *The Daughters of England* (1845). The absent volume, the female group which is not there, is the spinsters of England. Their erasure is explained in the Preface to *Mothers*:

> It was originally my intention to have added to the present work, a chapter of hints for Stepmothers, and another on the consolations of Old Maids, which I am far from believing to be few; but the subject more immediately under consideration grew from its importance to the usual extent of a book . . . and it grew also upon my own mind, as the duties and responsibilities of a mother were gradually unfolded, to an aspect of such solemn, profound, and immeasurable interest that I feel the more forcibly how inadequate are my feeble representations to do justice to the claims of society upon the devoted, conscientious, and persevering exertions of the Mothers of England.

The failure of this passage to complete the excuse for the absent chapters enacts the social invisibility of 'old maids' (or to translate into the implied negative, non-nubile virgins) as it and they disappear in a cloud of praise to motherhood. The power of the negative is also evident in Ellis' classic description of 'woman' as one 'whose deepest enjoyments are all relative; who has nothing, and is nothing of herself; whose experience, if unparticipated, is a total blank' (Ellis 1845: 161). The radical implications of this negation, this total blankness (on which men write what they wish to read), are lost on Ellis, who fails to see how they undermine her account of 'woman' as guardian of morals and ultimate purifier. The negative compromises all such claims.

Negation used in a different way is a prominent element in the language in which Dickens represents women. When he is dealing with areas, such as their sexuality, which are subject to powerful linguistic taboo, one can deal with his negatives as Freud in the essay on 'Negation' claimed to treat his patients' denials by interpreting them as 'a way of taking cognisance of what is repressed':

> In our interpretation, we take the liberty of disregarding the negation and of picking out the subject-matter alone of the association. It is as though the patient had said: 'It's true that my mother came into my

mind as I thought of this person, but I don't feel inclined to let the association count.' (in Strachey 1961: 235)

This will be demonstrated most extensively in the treatment of non-adulteresses in chapter 5. It is such features of Dickens' language, which are to be found in his construction of gender, that are to be established and explored. I shall now describe a framework in which to do this.

The semantic field: women as signs

So far it has been argued that it is appropriate for feminists concerned with the construction of gender in the nineteenth-century novel to address themselves to language, not directly to social conditions. Specifically, this means in the first instance considering what can be called the semantic field relating to women: all those groupings of women under linguistic signs (with their characteristic significances) that can be distinguished in Dickens' novels. A parallel would be the anthropologist's consideration of the linguistic terms for kinship (and their significances) in a given social group. In both these fields the critic is confronted by referents (or physical entities) and the linguistic signs to which they relate. But the relationship is not a simple one in which the referent is to be regarded as the meaning of the sign.

As already indicated, Ellis, in her sociological account (which none the less draws on the same system of representation as Dickens), relates her divisions of the field of feminine gender to marital and familial status: *wives, mothers, daughters* are subsumed into a super-ordinate category *women*. For her purposes the first three groups are treated as discrete, a fact symbolised physically by her separate volumes. Any assumption that this is somehow a direct reflection of actuality, an account of the species, is removed by the immediate recognition that any wife may be a mother and a daughter (a sentence that can be rewritten twice more with the key nouns redistributed). These are Ellis' signs, not labels over facts. And there is no reason to assume that an individual novelist's grouping/perception of those categories would be necessarily the same as hers. This is obviously true of Dickens' novels, where the shifting familial identity of female characters is particularly obvious, from Little Nell mothering her grandfather, Agnes Wickfield combining maternal, sisterly and marital roles towards David Copperfield, to Bella Wilfer, simultaneously mother and partner to her father, drawing him after her secret wedding into a *ménage à trois* in which he will not 'lose' her, by a revised wedding ceremony:

> 'But you know you are not [broken-hearted]; don't you, poor dear Pa? You know that you have only made a new relation who will be as fond of you and as thankful to you – for my sake and your own sake both – as I am; don't you, dear little Pa? Look here, Pa!' Bella put her finger on her own lip, and then on Pa's, then on her own lip again, and then on her husband's. 'Now we are a partnership of three, dear Pa.' (*Our Mutual Friend*, p. 668)

I have tried elsewhere (Ingham 1989) to distinguish Hardy's perception of this same semantic field, to show how for him there is an important and idiosyncratic overlap between signs for women and those for certain male figures: poor men and artists. Similarly, it is necessary to analyse the way in which Dickens divides up into signs the semantic field relating to women, if a precise reading of his account of gender is to be achieved. This will reveal the significance of the division into those particular signs and the implicit evaluation that he attaches to certain groups of women. These evaluations become even clearer and more meaningful when the question is asked: what is the superordinate or inclusive term corresponding to Ellis' term *women*? Since we can identify the inclusive or superordinate colour for *scarlet*, *crimson* and *vermilion* etc. as *red*, we are enabled to identify the constitutive features which are common to them all. In the same way, by examining in chapter 6 the nature of the larger group to which all Dickens' positively valued women belong and from which all his disvalued women are excluded, we are able to understand better how the system of evaluation works.

I propose, then, to examine Dickens' representations of women in terms of the signs within that field in relation to both gender and class. However, it is also necessary to discuss the signs in relation to the narrative sequences in which they occur. Novelistic signs are sometimes treated as though their meaning depended entirely on their own signification, when in fact it is partly determined by narrative patterns.

Narrative patterns: syntax and parataxis

In general, narratives purport to enact a struggle by narrators to appropriate sequences of events under explanations already, for the tellers, in place. So Dickens' narrator in *Edwin Drood* reporting Mrs Crisparkle's adverse judgement of Neville Landless ascribes it to women's (presumably well-known) admired and 'curious power of divining the characters of men, which would seem to be innate and instinctive' (p. 76). He then quickly demolishes the apparent merits of this female faculty by adding a modification that can be drawn from the assumed facts by one of his discernment:

> But it has not been quite so often remarked that this power . . . is for the most part absolutely incapable of self-revision; and that when it has delivered an adverse opinion which by all human lights is subsequently proved to have failed, it is undistinguishable from prejudice, in respect of its determination not to be corrected. (*Edwin Drood* p. 76)

An accumulation of such explanations can add up throughout a novel to one or more general laws to which events relate. One differentiating feature of individual novelists might be the nature of their attitude to this kind of appropriation, which will of course differ from novel to novel as well. The characteristic stance of Jane Austen's narrators, apart from those in *Mansfield Park* and *Persuasion*, seems to be one of effortless understanding of all events. Hardy's narrators, on the other hand, appear to be engaged in a desperate struggle to make sense of the incomprehensible. The nature of narratorial explanation in Dickens' novels is different from these two. All may be known but not all is construed. The narrator of *Oliver Twist* certainly works with the explanatory idea expressed in the Preface to the third edition that in Oliver himself is to be seen 'the principle of Good surviving through every adverse circumstance, and triumphing at last' (Clarendon edition, p. lxii). *Great Expectations* focuses around a complex moralised account of how a human personality matures. But even in these sample novels events stray beyond the narrator's power to confine them: the jollifications in Fagin's kitchen take on a playful cosiness at odds with its characterisation as a form of hell; the violent figure of Orlick is only loosely connected in syntactic terms with the rest of the plot, though his attacks on Mrs Joe and on Pip give him centrality. The containment of social issues within a rigid plot structure in *Hard*

Times is not matched in later novels like *Little Dorrit* and *Bleak House*, where, as I shall later show, ambiguity becomes a source of power.

Sometimes, also, interwoven with the actual plot of a novel may be other 'ghost' plots, as Gillian Beer calls them in *Darwin's Plots* (1983: 240). These are possible outcomes evoked for the reader by the desires, ambitions or future plans of the characters. So, for instance, one could describe as a ghost plot (in linguistic terms a *subjunctive* one) the story of a benign Miss Havisham and a loving Estella that Pip wishes so ardently to materialise for himself in *Great Expectations*. It is this unfulfilled dream which lends irony to the actual (or *indicative*) story in which he finds himself embroiled, with a benefactor, Magwitch, who is a criminal on the run. As will be seen in chapter 5, things which might have happened and are written in as possibilities, but which do not occur, can become in Dickens a powerful source of meaning which is not always as carefully controlled as in *Great Expectations*. They subvert rather than underpin the actual plots.

By the time of *Martin Chuzzlewit*, Dickens himself was providing simple guides to how to read the text: he wrote it, he said, with 'the design of exhibiting, in various aspects the commonest of vices', selfishness (Clarendon edition, p. 846). And later he wrote of *Dombey and Son*:

> I design to show Mr. D. with that one idea of the Son taking firmer and firmer possession of him, and swelling and bloating his pride to a prodigious extent. . . . So I mean to carry the story on, through all the branches and offshoots and meanderings that come up. (Clarendon edition, pp. xiv–xv)

What Dickens is suggesting here and elsewhere is what might be called a lateral or paratactic reading: one which ignores linear sequence to see events and characters as paralleling and throwing light on one another. Where syntax describes linear sequence, parataxis refers to constructions linked solely through juxtaposition. So in *Martin Chuzzlewit* selfishness is to be read through unrelated and (dis)similar manifestations; and the refusal of fatherhood in *Dombey and Son* through true fathers, false mothers, true mothers in that text.

The suggested method of reading paratactically in fact offers itself with all multiplot novels, where the form necessarily poses the question asked (and misleadingly answered) in *Bleak House*:

> What connexion can there be, between the place in Lincolnshire, the house in town, the Mercury in powder, and the whereabouts of Jo the

outlaw with the broom, . . . ? What connexion can there have been
between many people in the innumerable histories of this world, who,
from opposite sides of great gulfs, have, nevertheless, been very
curiously brought together! (p. 219)

Writing on such multiple plot structures, Garrett reviews several
approaches to what I am calling syntax and parataxis in narratives.
He sees them as single and dual focus structures showing 'the
centripetal impulse that organizes narrative around the development
of a protagonist and the impulse that elaborates an inclusive pattern
of simultaneous relationships' (Garrett 1980: 10). He elaborates on
the nature of the second impulse as it is commonly perceived: 'The use
of pictorial or spatial metaphors is common in discussions of multiple
narrative. . . . They represent the effort to spatialize narrative, to
rearrange its elements into atemporal categories such as patterns of
similarity and difference' (1980: 4). As he rightly adds, every narrative lends itself to this sort of reading but those which show 'the
inevitable discontinuity of multiple narratives' (*ibid.*) do so more than
the others. Garrett's concern is to argue that even in multiplot novels
the reader is presented with a double logic, a dialogue of both
structural principles, not the predominance of one over the other. For
my purposes it is enough to recognise that Dickens' novels use both
syntactic and paratactic forms of story-telling.

The implications of the juxtaposed sequences in Dickens, however,
are important: that many elements remain out of control. They defy
both narratorial explanation or justification and the will to shape
events evinced by the characters. Events, as in a medieval romance,
have primacy over people: they are, like Krook's combustion,
spontaneous. The consequences of this for the linguistic framework
are twofold. First, that individuals are presented as trapped in a world
of relatively autonomous happenings: men are only *ad hoc* agents who,
like Nickleby overthrowing Squeers, can intermittently act to control
events; women are not agents at all but the objects of men's small
actions and of circumstance. Second, the only recurrent overall
syntactic pattern is that described by Catherine Belsey in her influential *Critical Practice* (1980) as typical of what she calls the
'classic realist narrative': the final 'reinstatement of order' through
devices like marriage, decisive choices or the solution of a mystery
such as murder. This kind of reinstatement at the end of a novel is a
way of asserting tacitly that there is a natural law which states that,

without disturbing the status quo, 'a harmonious and coherent world' will *always* restore itself (Belsey 1980: 240). Given this constant overall framework, then, dealing with Dickens' narrative syntax usually means discussing only fragmentary sequences of events within it. It is the juxtaposed sequences discussed above that sometimes disturb the implications of the classic pattern.

Subsequent chapters will deal with signs and narrative syntax taken together, allowing the novels themselves to suggest how the signs representing women are to be distinguished. In the process five signs emerge: *nubile girl, fallen girl, excessive female, passionate woman* and the superordinate or inclusive term *'true' mother*. Analysis of the deep structure of these signs and their characteristic narrative patterns of syntax in fact reveals contradictory fears and desires which necessitate at surface level the eccentric divisions into which Dickens divides the semantic field relating to women. Close readings will show that Dickens' treatment of them is shot through with contradictions, which generate the unease that energises many of the texts. The contradictions themselves also represent the beginning of a shift in the signification of these signs, unexpected in a supposedly conventional writer. Such shifts are most obvious in the signs for sexually deviant women (the *fallen girl* and the *passionate woman*) on which Dickens' imagination, like that of many others in the nineteenth century, is powerfully at work. Their stories serve strikingly to transform his characteristically impersonal and reflexive narrative sentence (in which 'order restores itself') by briefly reclaiming agency for these women. It is a sexualised status which seems to be the necessary trigger for autonomous action. Paradoxically, however, his most highly valued nubile girls turn out to have, in context, as chapter 6 will show, the most disturbing and subversive effect of all. This is the most striking feature of his novelistic language: that it is the elaborately 'ideal' figures who undermine the very social structure that they are supposed to sustain. Finally, the Postscript will reconsider the traditional practice of locating stereotypes in Dickens' own life (what Slater (1983) calls 'Experience into art'), and suggests a reversal of the view that such accounts offer.

Chapter 2

Nubile girls

Appearances and their signification

In considering the range of signs deployed by Dickens in his representations of women the traditional course is to assume a category 'heroines'. Titles do claim heroes for eight of his major novels: *Pickwick Papers, Oliver Twist, Nicholas Nickleby, Barnaby Rudge, Martin Chuzzlewit, Dombey and Son, David Copperfield* and *The Mystery of Edwin Drood*. Only one, *Little Dorrit*, suggests that this is a novel with a heroine, and even here there is a significant refusal to name Amy rather than describe her as perceived by others. However, hero(es)/heroine(s) in the sense of 'chief protagonists, main agents', because of the narrative syntax outlined in chapter 1, which denies individuals the ability to control events, are hard to find. Perhaps only the two first-person narratives, *David Copperfield* and *Great Expectations*, qualify in this sense of *Bildungsroman*.

An alternative method to that of using titles as directives (which is notoriously misleading for many texts) is that of attaching the term heroine to the female sought for by the reader and identified as marriageable: the one who is distinctly written in as likely to be married in the closing chapters. Central figures in a Vatican Conclave are recognised as *papabile*; central female figures in many Victorian novels are recognised as *nubile*. Once this feature is spotted their identity becomes clear, as does its dependence on their sexual status as virgins. This does not mean that they necessarily marry in the course of the story. Like Nell Trent (or Maggie Tulliver) they may die

17

instead in some suitable way. It is the expectation that counts. For this reason I give the name *nubile girl* to this sign in Dickens' language. As will be shown, its signification relates to the insistence on nubility as well as to the passivity (suggested by the form of the adjective) shown by the women in the wooing and marrying process that they are expected to undergo. 'Girl' refers, of course, to their extreme youth.

The nature of the nubile girl's passivity is further delineated by Ellis. The required cause for this characteristic is the 'delicacy' which, according to her, 'forms so important a part of good taste, that where it does not exist as a natural instinct, it is taught as the first principle of good manners' (Ellis 1845: 178). Its essence is absence, ignorance, negation of sexuality:

> Nor can this, the greatest charm of female character, if totally neg-
> lected in youth, ever be acquired in afterlife. When the mind has been
> accustomed to what is vulgar, or gross, the fine edge of feeling is gone,
> and nothing can restore it. It is comparatively easy, on first entering
> upon life, to maintain the page of thought unsullied, by closing it
> against every improper image; but when once such images are allowed
> to mingle with the imagination, so as to be constantly revived by
> memory, and thus to give their tone to the habitual mode of thinking
> and conversing, the beauty of the female character may indeed be said
> to be gone, and its glory departed. (Ellis 1845: 178–9)

Paradoxically, then, the essential characteristics of figures in Dickens' novels such as Rose Maylie, Kate Nickleby, Madeline Bray, Emma Haredale, Mary Graham, Ruth Pinch, Florence Dombey, Dora Spenlow, Agnes Wickfield, Ada Clare, Esther Summerson, Amy Dorrit, Bella Wilfer, Lizzie Hexam and Rosa Bud are that they are identified by the text as marriageable virgins and also as having no knowledge of their attractiveness and its possible consequences. For the blank page to remain 'unsullied' they must avoid not only experience but knowledge.

Current codes of representation primarily attach signification to the age and appearance of women; Dickens does the same, though his semantics are different. With the nubile girl there is an over-insistence on lack of physicality in respect of female characteristics. The group already listed tends towards a pre-pubertal look. Rose Maylie is 'cast in so slight and exquisite a mould' (*Oliver Twist*, p. 187); Kate Nickleby appears as a girl of seventeen, the same age as Rose, 'slight but very beautiful' (p. 23), an interesting disjunction; Emma

Haredale in *Barnaby Rudge* is 'delicately shaped' (p. 155); Mary Graham is the preferred age and 'short in stature': 'her figure was slight, as became her years; but all the charms of youth and maidenhood set it off' (*Martin Chuzzlewit*, p. 28); Ruth Pinch in the same novel is 'slight and short' (p. 136). This emphasis on 'slightness', which may be paraphrased as 'absence of contour', illuminates the use of 'littleness' and in particular the adjective 'little', which appears to be almost in free variation with 'slight'. Littleness is a dominant characteristic of Nell Trent, Dora Spenlow and Amy Dorrit, and figures frequently in descriptions of girls like Agnes Wickfield, Esther Summerson and Ada Clare, among others. It cloaks the asexual implications of 'slight' under reassuring overtones of domesticity; *the/my little woman* for 'wife' had been in use since the seventeenth century. It is also reductive in force, given the long history of *little* as a patronising or playful way of describing people or things.

Few nubile girls are older than twenty and even fewer avoid littleness, apart from Lizzie Hexam in a plot which requires her to row a boat, and the androgynous Helena Landless in *The Mystery of Edwin Drood*. It even infects the vigorous Bella Wilfer once she has sullied her blank page by marrying John Rokesmith (né Harmon), presumably as a heavy-handed narratorial attempt to reinstate her innocence. She becomes Harmon's 'little wife' who lays her 'little right hand' on his eyes to tell him in the obliquest possible terms of their future 'little baby' (*Our Mutual Friend*, p. 688). At the other extreme is Nell Trent, whose littleness truly marks her out as belonging to the group under discussion. It is not usual to include her amongst marriageable girls but this is because of a non-textual consideration of her that classifies her as child. That is not how the text reveals her. Despite (or because of) her pre-pubertal state, she is distinctively presented in the usual terms for this sign. She has the 'slightest' of figures and a very small and delicate frame, and she is irreproachably virgin, innocent and ignorant. From the start, however, she is regarded as potentially nubile by her brother, Fred Trent, who solicits Dick Swiveller to plot for a marriage with her. Panders such as Trent are not uncommon companions for innocent girls in Dickens, as, for instance, the role Ralph Nickleby adopts towards his niece, Kate, shows. Later, in *The Old Curiosity Shop*, Nell is pursued by the dwarf Quilp, who desires her as a second wife and says so unequivocally. This inclusion of Nell in the representations of the sign in question is important for an understanding of the ultimately paradoxical significance that attaches to it.

The absence in these girls of the bodily contours that mark out a female is compensated for by metaphor. The straight lines are concealed under pictorial images that imply a celebration of what is viewed, but which really serve to deflect or diffuse attention. The most obvious of the images is the angel, which Michie describes as 'at once a metaphor for femininity and for cliché' (1987: 90). She characterises other uses that attempt to challenge the trope, but Dickens does not do this. In his work the angel is merely a rewriting of bodilessness. Rose Maylie is 'at that age, when, if ever angels be for God's good purposes enthroned in mortal forms, they may be, without impiety, supposed to abide in such as hers' (*Oliver Twist*, p. 187). The conditional nature of the identification adds a sense of impermanence even to this degree of physicality for Rose. Later when she is on the brink of total physical disintegration Harry Maylie again eulogizes her as 'one of God's own angels, fluttered between life and death' (p. 232). Nell, achieving dissolution in an effortless angelic progress from life, evokes a similar comment from the narrator for her 'mild lovely look', scarcely focused by the comment that 'So shall we know the angels in their majesty, after death' (*The Old Curiosity Shop*, p. 539). Agnes is repeatedly seen by Copperfield as his 'good Angel' (p. 312), ancillary to him as a guardian angel is, and existing mainly in antithesis to his bad angel, Steerforth. Dora is his pagan angel, 'a Fairy, a Sylph' (p. 333). And when Lizzie Hexam bends over Betty Higden, the dying woman thinks 'all is over with me on earth, and this must be an Angel' (*Our Mutual Friend*, p. 512). Though sometimes described as 'the murder' of the body (Michie 1987: 90), the effect of the image of the angel in Dickens is rather to render the body amorphous.

Other images serve the same purpose as the angel: they replace female physicality with other physical referents and so reinforce the apparent asexuality. Since they are frequently drawn from the natural world they also reduce women to something less than human; and since they are characteristically generic rather than specific, they imply a unitary female nature. In *Oliver Twist*, the first of many Roses weeps into a flower, and 'it seemed as though the outpouring of her fresh young heart, claimed kindred with the loveliest things in nature' (p. 232). Florence Dombey at the Skettles' party is, bathetically, 'the beautiful little rosebud of the room' (p. 198). Lady Dedlock's maid, another Rose, with a 'rosy and yet delicate bloom', has drops of rain on her hair 'like the dew upon a flower fresh gathered' (*Bleak House*, pp. 85–6). The last rose, Rosa Bud, is also a well that has never been moved (*Edwin Drood*, pp. 62–3) and Copperfield's Dora is repeatedly his blossom. Women are concealed beneath generic flowers, conventionally sparkling water, hazily unspecific blossom. Or they take on the role of household pets: Emma Haredale and Dolly Varden are doves or caged birds, depending on circumstance; Rosa Bud is alternatively 'Pussy'; Esther Summerson is happy to describe herself as 'a mouse' (*Bleak House*, p. 112); Fanny sees Amy Dorrit as a 'Dormouse' and a 'Tortoise' (pp. 584 and 586); and Dora Spenlow certainly treats Jip as though they were peers. Agnes Wickfield on the other hand is dehumanised to the extreme of becoming an unspecified 'stained-glass window' (*David Copperfield*, pp. 191, 435, 659).

The process of substituting other signifiers goes still further in Dickens' language, as in some contemporaries', where the kind of imagery just described extends into a series that fragments women into so many pieces. Emma Haredale and Dolly Varden walking on a breezy terrace at first become, in the familiar kind of imagery, cultivated blooms whose very conventionality is laboured: 'there are no flowers for any garden like such flowers, let horticulturalists say what they may' (*Barnaby Rudge*, p. 155). But later the two women disintegrate into the stock components of a summer's day: 'Light hearts, light hearts, that float so gaily on a smooth stream, that are so sparkling and buoyant in the sunshine – down upon fruit, bloom upon flowers, blush in summer air, life of the winged insect whose whole existence is a day' (*Barnaby Rudge*, p. 544). Dora Spenlow is even more diffused by transposition into serial images: 'The sun shone Dora, and the birds sang Dora. The south wind blew Dora, and the wild flowers in the hedges were all Doras, to a bud' (*David Copperfield*, p. 412). The linguistic structure of this passage enacts Dora's displacement, as the object status she is given in the second and fourth clause is lost by her relegation to the tertiary role in the first and third: woman is seen not as subject nor even as object but as adverb. Though 'idealised' she does not matter.

Fragmentation or 'morselisation' of women, as Tanner (1979: 349ff.) calls a similar process in *Madame Bovary* (1857), becomes a more distinctive feature of Dickens' language because of two other devices that work in the same way: the use of the (literal) part for the whole and the extension of that use into description by inventory. Just as current language allowed the substitution of 'hands' for 'factory workers' so it also allowed for the replacement of 'women' by 'petticoats': working men as machine-pushers, women as garments. Strikingly on this linguistic pattern is Dickens' description of Lizzie Hexam. It is the predatory Eugene Wrayburn who perceives her as 'the lonely girl with the dark hair' (*Our Mutual Friend*, p. 163), and on closer inspection as 'a deep rich piece of colour' (p. 164). Lizzie is designated, as Bassein says of other such expressions, as 'less than whole, less than total, less than complete' (Bassein 1984: p. 3). The fact that the phrase used of Lizzie is visually striking makes it more, not less, reductive. She exists only as this single perception of Wrayburn's; his glance creates her.

Where one man creates a woman as a single 'piece of colour', another extends his gaze and turns metonymy into inventory. Women as catalogues of desired physical attributes have a long history in literary representations. They occur at least as early as Chaucer's eulogy of Blanche in *The Book of the Duchess* and were common enough for Olivia in *Twelfth Night* to parody what she expects the gazing male to make of her beauty: 'I will give out divers schedules of my beauty. It shall be inventoried, and every particle and utensil labell'd to my will: as – item, two lips indifferent red; item, two grey eyes with lids to them; item, one neck, one chin, and so forth' (I.5.229ff.). The generic nature of the items described is frequent and it is characteristic of Dickens. Ruth Pinch surrendering to John Westlock is a typical example: 'The soft, light touch fell coyly, but quite naturally, upon the lover's shoulder; the delicate waist, the drooping head, the blushing cheek, the beautiful eyes, the exquisite little mouth itself, were all as natural as possible' (*Martin Chuzzlewit*, p. 814). Ruth is a random and incomplete listing of hand, waist, head, cheek and eyes, no longer hers but the possessions of Westlock and the narrator, for whom their unspecific nature as the normal attributes of the nubile girl is characterised by the definite article. In such lists *her* is regularly replaced not only by *the*, but also by *a* or zero. Amy Dorrit has 'a delicately bent head, a tiny form, a quick little pair of busy hands, and a shabby dress' (p. 53); Ada Clare is perceived by Esther (in her role of surrogate male) with 'such rich golden hair, such soft blue eyes, and such a bright, innocent, trusting face' (*Bleak House*, p. 29).

This last inclusion of dress along with physical attributes has the same result as when Pope in *The Rape of the Lock* places the 'Bibles' among the puffs, patches, powders and other objects on Belinda's dressing table. The two things are equated: clothes become part of the body and vice versa (which is why letting down the hair can be used as a form of undressing). Though Dickens, as is well known, often blurred the line between people and things, this particular example of his practice was not peculiar to him, but part of a wider linguistic convention challenged by later novelists. However, it was a particularly natural idiom for Dickens to adopt in his representations of women, with the line between body and garment blurred. Significantly, the catalogue that is Dolly Varden is perceived in this fuzzy way by the infatuated Simon Tappertit:

> she was . . . the very pink and pattern of good looks, in a smart little cherry-coloured mantle, with a hood of the same drawn over her head, and upon the top of that hood, a little straw hat trimmed with cherry-coloured ribbons, and worn the merest trifle on one side – just enough in short to make it the wickedest and most provoking head-dress that ever malicious milliner devised. And not to speak of the manner in which these cherry-coloured decorations brightened her eyes . . . she wore such a cruel little muff, and such a heart-rending pair of shoes. (*Barnaby Rudge*, p. 149)

This elaboration on Dolly as petticoat carries, unusually, the implication that this is not only how male eyes see her but also how she sees herself and how she wishes to be seen. For her, as for her admirer, clothes have equal status with her body as the weapons of provocative cruelty and of the wish to rend hearts. But then Dolly is only a shadow or false nubile girl. As the daughter of a locksmith and therefore of a lower class than Emma Haredale, niece of the squire, she serves a useful purpose when both of them are kidnapped by lustful rioters. She is the scapegoat who carries the necessary burden of sexual attractiveness: she is indelicately 'plump' whereas Emma is 'delicately shaped' (p. 155). Where Emma is virtually invisible, Dolly is a suitable target for the greedy male eyes: 'what mortal eyes could have avoided wandering to the delicate boddice, the streaming hair, the neglected dress, the perfect abandonment and unconsciousness of the blooming little beauty?' (*Barnaby Rudge*, pp. 455–6). Dolly is declassed by her own physicality.

But even Dora Spenlow, who unlike Dolly Varden can be assumed to provoke an admiring male obsession with her body unwittingly, is dehumanised by an inventory that gives priority to clothes. Copperfield remembers her nostalgically as 'a straw hat and blue ribbons, and a quantity of curls, and . . . two slender arms, against a bank of blossom and bright leaves' (p. 338). Later, just before the wedding, she is entirely represented in their new house by this blue-ribboned garden-hat.

The nubile girl, so often presumed to be idealised, is a sign denied sexuality, physicality and individuality, and reductively treated in terms of surfaces and displaced physical appearance. The method uniformly suggests, without achieving, eulogy. Perfection is assumed but never demonstrated. However, the assumption presupposes a match between beauty and character, particularly when the face is involved. But with Dora, for instance, Copperfield's disillusion seems to reside in a sense that he has been cheated by her beauty into believing her to be other than she is. And at the time when Dickens began to write novels a signifying code relating face to character was certainly available to him. As Fahnestock puts it: 'Readers from the 1850s through the 1870s could be relied on to understand something of the code of *physiognomy*, the "science" of reading character in the face' (1981: 325). With the translation of the essays of the Swiss writer, Johann Lavater, from the late eighteenth century onwards, the reading of faces began to be regarded as a science.

Typical of this approach is Alexander Walker's *Physiognomy Founded on Physiology* (1834). This work, set carefully on a framework of race, nationality, class and gender, groups together negroes and women as those in whom 'the sensations are strong . . . while the mental operations . . . are weak' (Walker 1834: 220). For Walker 'the first rule of physiognomy applicable to the face in particular, results from the examining of the predominance of . . . [the organs] of sense over those of volition, or *vice versa*' (p. 221). By volition he means will-power. Another general rule is that the eye and ear are 'intellectual organs', the nose and mouth 'animal organs'. Fullness of either lip, as in negroes, indicates voluptuousness or a facile nature (p. 257), an upturned nose that the owner has 'rapid impressions and emotions' or is even 'pert, impudent, indelicate or filthy' (p. 260). Dark eyes, since they indicate 'more accurate inspection and generally firmer character' are 'best suited to the male countenance', whereas light blue eyes indicate 'less accurate inspection and generally softer character' and so 'best suit the feminine countenance' (pp. 266–7). Walker gives detailed illustrations of different types of each facial feature and their implications for character.

On all this, with which he must have been familiar either from a knowledge of Lavater, referred to in *Our Mutual Friend* (p. 207), or the practice of his fellow writers or both, Dickens drew to some extent.

The one feature referred to repeatedly is the eyes of women, those irreproachably intellectual organs. Though several like Nell, Rose Maylie and Ada Clare have the less observant blue eyes suited to females, colour is often unspecified. Eyes are usually mentioned, but in general terms: Ruth Pinch's are merely 'beautiful', Dolly Varden's 'sparkling', Florence Dombey's 'constant'. Amy Dorrit is an exception with 'soft hazel eyes' and the usually anomalous Helena Landless has 'intense dark' ones (*Edwin Drood*, p. 69). Rosa Bud in the last novel has also, surprisingly, dark eyes, rendered feminine by their 'pouting' appearance (p. 22) suggestive in Walker's terms of too rapid reactions and emotions (Walker 1834: 265).

For the rest, the distinguishing characteristic of Dickens' language is the absence of details relating to those animal organs, the mouth and nose, apart from the occasional pouting in Dora or Rosa Bud. This paucity of facial detail represents a significant variation on the developing practice in novels from 1830 onwards for more detail to be given and decoded by the narrator. This absence leaves mainly general outlines, falling within the physiognomists' limits of what was most suitable in a woman's face as a reflection of traditional female virtues, which can be filled in to create the beholder's own version of feminine perfection. The same scope is left by what I have called the generic imagery. In the last (unfinished) novel Dickens presents as comic Edwin Drood's ability to overwrite his unwilling fiancée Rosa Bud with the physical and facial characteristics of his ideal fiancée:

'Tall?'
'Immensely tall!' Rosa being short.
'Must be gawky, I should think?' . . .
'I beg your pardon; not at all. . . . What is termed a fine woman; a splendid woman.'
'Big nose, no doubt,' . . .
'Not a little one certainly,' is the quick reply. (Rosa's being a little one.)
'Long pale nose, with a red knob in the middle. *I* know the sort of nose,' . . .
'You *don't* know the sort of nose, Rosa . . . because it's nothing of the kind.'
'Not a pale nose, Eddy?'
'No.' . . .
'A red nose. Oh! I don't like red noses. However . . . she can always powder it.'
'She would scorn to powder it,' says Edwin, becoming heated. (*Edwin Drood*, pp. 20–1)

What would now be described as the 'writable' representation of feminine appearance was one which, as Fahnestock (1981: 328) points out, was recommended by Leigh Hunt in his 'Criticism on feminine beauty':

> It has been justly observed, that heroines are best painted in general terms, as in *Paradise Lost*:
>
>   Grace was in all her steps, heaven in her eye, etc. or by some striking instance of the effects of their beauty, as in Homer, where old age itself is astonished at the sight of Helen, and does not wonder that Paris has brought a war on his country for her sake. Particular description divides the opinion of the readers and may offend some of them. The most elaborate portrait of the heroine of Italian romance could say nothing for her, compared with the distractions that she caused to so many champions. (Hunt 1825: 71–2).

Hunt's second point here (unnoticed by Fahnestock, who quotes only part of the above passage) that heroines are perceived as effects/affects is a relevant one for Dickens to which I shall return in chapter 6.

Given this ability of men to write in their preferred woman, women can be said to be 'unceasingly iterable' (Michie 1987: 89). This idea throws new light on the assertion of the texts that for all these nubile girls part of their signification is a unique perfection; since what makes it unique are the preferences of an individual male. The contradiction is repeated across the whole range of Dickens' novels. But viewing the fiction as a whole, one can discern in an early story in *Sketches by Boz* a paratactic comment on Dickens' own methods of representing women. In 'The four sisters' there is a strange account of the apparently communal wooing of the four:

> Now, where on earth the husband came from, by what feelings the poor man could have been actuated, or by what process of reasoning the four Miss Willises succeeded in persuading themselves that it was possible for a man to marry one of them, without marrying them all, are questions too profound for us to resolve: certain it is, however, that the visits of Mr. Robinson . . . were received – that the four Miss Willises were courted in due form by the said Mr. Robinson – that the neighbours were perfectly frantic in their anxiety to discover which of the four Miss Willises was the fortunate fair, and that the difficulty they experienced in solving the problem was not at all lessened by the announcement of the eldest Miss Willis, – '*We* are going to marry Mr. Robinson.' (pp. 14–15)

There follows an apparently communal wedding with all four sisters repeating the responses. The five settle down together and only a successful pregnancy finally distinguishes the youngest sister as the wife.

It is made clear throughout this suggestive narrative that it is not the man who is responsible for a delightfully ambiguous state of affairs offering triple and incestuous bigamy, but the sisters, who insist on their own interchangeability. All cats are grey in the dark because woman is unitary and wishes to be so. She can take on an *ad hoc* particularity only when a man rewrites her as Mrs Robinson and stamps her as his own by impregnation. Consequently, it can be seen that the 'idealised' heroines of Dickens' novels are representations of a contradictory kind whose ideality is a thin varnish.

Three other episodes in the novels, juxtaposed with the narratives involving nubile girls, make similar paratactic comments on male authors' reworkings of stock descriptions of women. They enlarge the point that Walter Bagehot made in 1858, when he wrote derisively that 'most men can make a jumble of blue eyes and fair hair and pearly teeth, that does very well for a young lady' (in Collins 1971: 396). Momentarily in Dickens such representations are, surprisingly, questioned, in gratuitous episodes relating to the artistic description of women.

The earliest is Miss La Creevy's grotesque painting of beautiful Kate Nickleby. The artist is seen as intent on infusing 'into the counterfeit countenance of Miss Nickleby by a bright salmon flesh-tint' a fine artistic effect 'which she had originally hit upon while executing the miniature of a young officer' (*Nicholas Nickleby*, p. 114). The subordination of the sitter to the medium and the medium to the male is made in a condensed dream-work fashion. Less oblique is the satirical citation of a 'glowing passage' of novelistic language describing a heroine that Miss Twinkleton censors while reading aloud to Rosa Bud: ' "Ever dearest and best adored," ' – said Edward, clasping the dear head to his breast, and drawing the silken hair through his caressing fingers, from which he suffered it to fall like golden rain' (*Edwin Drood*, p. 202). The self-referentiality of a description involving a fetishistic head and hair (characterised by the use of a definite article instead of possessive *her*) becomes evident when the passage is read alongside an earlier scene in *Our Mutual Friend*. There Lizzie Hexam unpins the hair of Jenny Wren (alias Fanny Cleaver), the crippled dolls' dressmaker, so that it falls 'in a beautiful shower

over the poor shoulders that were much in need of such adorning rain'
(p. 347).

The most pointed example is also found in the same novel as the
Twinkleton passage where Rosa Bud, that most nubile of girls,
already introduced as the fiancée of Edwin Drood before she appears,
is first seen not in the flesh but in a portrait by her fiancé that hangs in
the house of the menacing and lustful John Jasper:

> Even when the sun shines brilliantly, it seldom touches the grand piano
> in the recess, or the folio music-books on the stand, or the book-shelves
> on the wall, or the unfinished picture of a blooming schoolgirl hanging
> over the chimneypiece; her flowing brown hair tied with a blue riband,
> and her beauty remarkable for a quite childish, almost babyish touch
> of saucy discontent, comically conscious of itself. (There is not the least
> merit in this picture which is a mere daub; but it is clear that the painter
> has made it humourously – one might almost say revengefully – like the
> original.) (p. 7)

Rosa is already an artefact, the last in a series of objects along with
piano, music books and bookshelves. She has further been reduced
within this artefact to a stereotypical schoolgirl by one man (who has
vengefully rewritten her within the genre as discontented and self-
conscious) and then appropriated by another who wishes to possess
her. Momentarily, these three episodes work to question the conventional method of representing desirable women, even though the
point is not pursued. There is a discontinuity in the narrative syntax:
the usual point of view returns and events move on as if these aberrant
detours had never been made. However, their intermittent emergence
from below the surface is enough to destabilise in a disturbing way the
usual account of nubile girls in Dickens' novels.

Narrative syntax: the eating of marriageable girls

What has been said so far about the signification of Dickens' *nubile
girl* sign is only half the story, the familiar half that has been
critically mythologised as 'idealising'. It has been shown above how a
recognition of the disvaluing of women involved can demythologise
Dickens' representations and overthrow the assumption that they are
innocently ideal. But a further significance attaches to the sign that
enforces a rereading beyond this one. This new level of meaning

relates to an element vital in the vocabulary for the description of women during this period: that of hunger and food. Several critics, including Michie (1987), have explored in other texts the way that they code women's hunger and/or their relationship to food. It is a common language which is used to state both orthodoxies and challenges to them: both the positive statements and the health warnings.

The basis of the code is the importance in middle-class women's lives of the ordering, possibly preparation and serving, and certainly (formal) eating of food. Ellis, for instance, who takes the positive view, sees it as providing a means for women to fulfil themselves by nurturing others. They need to be 'acquainted with the best method of doing everything upon which domestic comfort depends' (Ellis 1845: 83). It is also a mild form of control within the household, as is clear from her recommendation that women should provide food according to a very fine calculation:

> With regard to food . . . I am inclined to think that to have a table comfortably supplied with a moderate variety of dishes, is by no means inconsistent with the strictest economy. I have sometimes even fancied that a spare dinner had the effect of producing a very disproportionate appetite. (Ellis 1843a: 284)

It is for her a basic part of a larger strategy which makes it also necessary to be good-tempered while 'cooking, broiling, stewing, and steaming . . . concocting good things' (Ellis 1843b: 335). A harmonious domestic balance will thus be maintained.

As for the woman herself, the preparation of food is symbolic of her essential abilities as contrasted with those of men. So much lies in the boiling of an egg:

> It is sometimes spoken of as a defect in women that they have less power of abstraction than men; and certainly if they were required to take part in all the occupations of the other sex, it would be so; but for my own part . . . I never could see it an advantage to any woman, to be capable of abstraction beyond a certain extent. It may be all very well for a man of science now and then to boil a watch instead of an egg for breakfast; but a woman . . . has no business to be so far absorbed in any purely intellectual pursuit, as not to know when water is boiling over the fire. (Ellis 1843b: 321–2)

The challenge to this orthodoxy, the rejection of the food-trap, comes from works like Florence Nightingale's 'Cassandra' (part of her *Suggestions for Thought to Searchers after Religious Truth*, written and revised 1852–9). In this she takes up the question of women's essential nature raised in the last quotation from Ellis. Given her social class, it is not unexpected that it is the ritual consumption of food rather than its preparation which for Nightingale symbolises oppression:

> Mrs. A has the imagination, the poetry of a Murillo, and has sufficient power of execution to show that she might have had a great deal more. Why is she not a Murillo? . . . If she has a knife and fork in her hands during three hours of the day, she cannot have a pencil or a brush. Dinner is the great sacred ceremony of the day, the great sacrament. To be absent from dinner is equivalent to being ill. Nothing else will excuse us from it. (Stark 1979: 30–1)

For Nightingale such meals are the hours on a clock of servitude: she sees women like herself measuring out this life by the intervals 'from breakfast till dinner, from dinner till tea' (in Stark 1979: 35–6). Work is precluded because every husband thinks 'he would not have so good a dinner' if it were undertaken (p. 44). In her idiolect such meals become a poison relentlessly administered every day, while lack of intellectual nourishment, withheld because of the claims of routine, causes starvation.

For Nightingale the idea of the family meal as forcible poisoning was so firmly established that she uses it as the vehicle of an image expressing her horror at the need to submit to another domestic torture – being read aloud to, the most miserable exercise of the human intellect:

> It is like lying on one's back, with one's hands tied and having liquid poured down one's throat. Worse than that, because suffocation would immediately ensue and put a stop to this operation. But no suffocation would stop the other. (Stark 1979: 34)

Women's relationship to food, then, is likely to figure in some strongly positive or negative form in Victorian accounts of them and their signification/what they stand for. Dickens' is no exception. His novelistic idiolect presents the reader with variations on Ellis' position: that for women to provide and/or dispense food is a sign that the natural order of things is being maintained. This can be simply illustrated by reference to basic providers like the wet-nurse in *Dombey and Son*, Polly Toodle (who has already produced an 'apple-cheeked' family) or to Mrs Bagnet in *Bleak House*, of whom Mr George says warmly 'I never saw her, except upon a baggage-waggon, when she wasn't washing greens!' (p. 382). It is presumably, on the other hand, the absence of a true woman in Dombey's house that results after his first wife's funeral in 'a cold collation, set forth in a cold pomp of glass and silver, and looking more like a dead dinner lying in state than a social refreshment' (p. 60). The subliminal equation of the late Mrs Dombey and the dead dinner suggests the socially refreshing value of a live woman as the accompaniment to food. Such a role is given to Bella Wilfer when in a later novel she transforms her father's wretched meal of bread and milk by her presence (*Our Mutual Friend*, pp. 605ff.).

But nubile girls are more than comforting companions at a meal for Dickens. As a contemporary noticed in 1870: 'Mr. Dickens could not get over the notion that a love scene is a rich and luscious sort of juice, to be sucked up in the sort of way in which a bowl of punch and a Christmas dinner are so often enjoyed in his tales.' Dickens' obsession with food generally, especially as an occasion of or source for male conviviality, is a point well taken. As the reviewer goes on to make clear, however, he is referring specifically to scenes where women are involved, for he continues:

> all beauty, all that he thinks loveable, is apt to be treated by him as if it were a pot of raspberry jam, something luscious to the palate, instead of something fascinating to the imagination and those finer powers by which harmony of expression is perceived. (Collins 1971: 549)

This captures precisely a displacement onto food, with which, as will be shown, nubile girls are equated, giving them that lusciousness denied to them in descriptions of their physical appearance. They are angels, flowers, buds to the eye but raspberry jam, roast goose, steak pie, sauce or turkish delight to the palate. It is by these affects/effects that their meaning is revealed.

As early as *Sketches by Boz* the connection between attractive young women and food begins to be made in, for instance, the person of Mrs Chirrup. Food surrounds her as it does many women, because she is 'an incomparable housewife', a bathetic accolade that Ellis would have entirely approved: 'In all the arts of domestic arrangement and management, in all the mysteries of confectionery-making, pickling, and preserving, never was such a thorough adept as that nice little body.' Her nice little body is immediately placed in close proximity to the succulent roast goose that she carves. The admiration expressed for both inevitably suggests parallels:

The legs of the bird slide gently down into a pool of gravy, the wings seem to melt from the body, the breast separates into a row of juicy slices, the smaller and more complicated parts of his anatomy are perfectly developed, a cavern of stuffing is revealed, and the goose is gone! (*Sketches by Boz*, pp. 585–6).

Periodically, direct statements *are* made in which women are equated with food; and their recurrence provides a frame of reference to which all women–food involvements relate. Such a statement is made, for instance, in the account of Ruth Pinch making a steak pie for her brother, Tom, and turning herself at the same time into the crowning touch to a gastronomic treat:

It was a perfect treat . . . to see her with her brows knit, and her rosy lips pursed up, kneading away at the crust, rolling it out, cutting it up into strips, lining the basin with it . . . chopping up the steak into small pieces . . . until, at last . . . she clapped her hands all covered with paste and flour, at Tom, and burst out heartily into such a charming little laugh of triumph, that the pudding need have no other seasoning to commend it to the taste of any reasonable man on earth. (*Martin Chuzzlewit*, pp. 601–2)

Ruth as seasoning to 'the unalloyed and perfect pudding' is matched by Ruth as sauce to Tom's earlier chops and potatoes: 'Surely she was the best sauce for chops ever invented. The potatoes seemed to take a pleasure in sending up their grateful steam before her; the froth upon the pint of porter pouted to attract her notice' (p. 585).

As Ruth becomes indistinguishable from sauce and porter beer from her, so at Bella Wilfer's wedding-breakfast Bella and Harmon's possession of her enhance the food itself. Everything is transformed, even whitebait, 'the dishes being seasoned with Bliss – an article which they are sometimes out of at Greenwich – were of perfect flavour' (*Our Mutual Friend*, p. 668). Rosa Bud, pink and greedy in the sweet shop that sells 'Lumps-of-Delight', is easy to mistake for such a lump as, licking her fingers, she seems to turn to self-consumption. In the shop she

begins to partake of it with great zest: previously taking off and rolling up a pair of little pink gloves, like rose-leaves, and occasionally putting her little pink fingers to her rosy lips, to cleanse them from the Dust of Delight that comes off the Lumps. (*Edwin Drood*, p. 20)

It is in *David Copperfield*, in an image as hyperbolic as Nightingale's forced-feeding image, that the edibility of a nubile girl is most directly stated when Copperfield dines for the first time with Dora Spenlow and her father: 'I have not the least idea what we had for dinner, besides Dora. My impression is, that I dined off Dora, entirely, and sent away half-a-dozen plates untouched' (p. 334). And at his wedding, as at Bella Wilfer's and Harmon's, food is similarly transformed, and he perceives himself 'eating and drinking . . . nothing but love and marriage' (p. 540).

Nubile girls are in this way translated into the male sensations attaching to consumption of delicious food at the same time that direct physicality is overtly denied them. Appearances declare them sexless, the food analogy defines them *only* as sexual objects, consumable by the watching male. And to add spice they are as titillatingly unaware as the raspberry jam, the goose, the steak pie that they are 'Lumps of Delight'. That the nature of the desired consumption is sexual is made clear by a series of recurrent narrative sequences in which they are characteristically involved. They have been written in as marriageable but marriage (apart from Dora Spenlow's, Lucie Manette's and Bella Wilfer's) is not what they engage in, except as an exit. Instead, they become enmeshed in fragments of narrative characterised by suspense. The dynamics of this depend on the tension involved in a developing male threat to an ignorant, innocent girl whose nature requires her not to understand it fully. The outcome is regularly the frustration of the threat by other means than hers. These passages represent the 'ghost' or subjunctive plots referred to in chapter 1 which blackly shadow actuality with the horrors that might have happened.

The opening section of *The Old Curiosity Shop* is a paradigm example. There is an obtrusive male narrator, Master Humphrey, who lays a voyeuristic stress on his fears for Nell Trent's safety at the same time as stressing her lack of contours and spiritual innocence in a typically inconsequential combination, 'so very young, so spiritual, so slight and fairy-like a creature' (p. 13). The fears are the more powerful for being nebulous. They hint at possible 'villainy of the worst kind' (p. 12) in her grandfather and they crystallise around the image of Nell in the curiosity shop 'surrounded and beset by everything that was foreign to its nature, and farthest removed from the sympathies of her sex and age' (p. 13). The reader is not told what exactly is foreign to, what furthest from the pre-pubertal Nell. But the narrator obsessively fills past, present and even future with variations on this imagined contrast as he visualises her 'holding her solitary way among a crowd of wild grotesque companions; the only pure, fresh, youthful object in the throng' (p. 13).

The elaboration of this classically Dickensian juxtaposition follows in a series of incidents which are all variations on the theme of the menaced girl. Before the first, the grotesque Quilp, when his wife says that if she were to die tomorrow he 'could marry anybody he pleased' (p. 32), actually threatens to eat her: ' "O you nice creature!" were the words with which he broke silence; smacking his lips as if this were no figure of speech, and she were actually a sweetmeat. "O you precious darling! Oh you de-licious charmer!" ' (p. 35). But what he would really like to eat, in his own particular way, is soon revealed in what follows later, to be Nell:

> 'There's no hurry, little Nell, no hurry at all,' said Quilp.
> 'How should you like to be my number two, Nelly?'
> 'To be what, sir?'
> 'My number two, Nelly; my second; my Mrs. Quilp,' said the dwarf. The child looked frightened, but seemed not to understand him . . .
> 'To be Mrs. Quilp the second, when Mrs. Quilp the first is dead, sweet Nell . . . to be my wife, my little cherry-cheeked, red-lipped wife. Say that Mrs. Quilp lives five years, or only four, you'll be just the proper age for me.' (p. 45)

He begins the process of consumption by kissing her with a smacking of the lips and the comment 'what a nice kiss that was – just upon the rosy part' (p. 72). He continues it, in imagination at least, by the relish of his description to her grandfather: 'She's so, . . . so small, so compact, so beautifully modelled, so fair, with such blue veins and such a transparent skin.' In sum, for him, though hardly for anyone else, she is 'such a chubby, rosy, cosy, little Nell' (p. 73).

Finally, in a third scene, the pattern of the threat to consume what is all the more desirable for her not understanding the nature of the menace is made plain: Quilp confesses to an interest in and designs on Nell's bed. Before he does so, however, he is described as 'drawing in his breath with great relish as if he were taking soup' (p. 85).

> 'Has she come to sit upon Quilp's knee . . . or is she going to bed in her own little room inside here? . . .'
> 'No,' – replied the child . . . 'never again! Never again!' . . .
> 'She's very sensitive. . . . Very sensitive; that's a pity. The bedstead is much about my size. I think I shall make it *my* little room.' (p. 86)

Nell's flight removes her from Quilp's grasp though she is still ignorant of his meaning. But the Nell–Quilp story is the blueprint for a recurrent type in which a girl, carrying the force of the 'unsullied page' – innocent both of understanding and experience – is threatened by illicit male desire. The blank is essential to the structure of the incidents which depend on the ever-increasing threat of its defilement.

But it is a threat which the narrator relishes, as is clear from the relatively extended treatments and the gratuitous repetition of his accounts. It is not enough for Kate Nickleby to be threatened once in this way; it happens several times. Early reference is made to the contrast between her 'gentle innocence' and the 'rugged villainy' of her uncle, Ralph Nickleby, a kind of half-hearted pander. For it is he who brings her first to the eyes of the dressmaker's husband, Mantalini, 'an odious man' in the state of half-undress indicated by a dressing gown (p. 125). Later he uses her as a sexual decoy for the rich young gull, Lord Frederick Verisopht, and so exposes her to the designs of his parasite and Verisopht's mentor, Sir Mulberry Hawk. Four scenes of menace follow each on the same pattern but with varying degrees of intensity.

In three of them a voyeuristic element is introduced by the way in which Hawk plays out his amorous pursuit of Kate for the benefit of the other men present, as he treats her like a woman of easy virtue masquerading as an innocent girl. The first verbal attack takes place in the drawing room before dinner and is well received by them:

> These gentlemen had not yet quite recovered the jest, when dinner was announced, and they were thrown into fresh ecstasies by a similar cause; for Sir Mulberry Hawk . . . shot dexterously past Lord Frederick Verisopht who was about to lead Kate downstairs, and drew her arm through his up to the elbow . . . and led Kate downstairs with an air of familiarity. (p. 236)

In the scene over the dinner-table, at which, significantly, Kate is trapped, Hawk continues his double role of persecuting her with his attentions and parodying his own behaviour for his male audience. Part of his attack is the pretence of her willing assent – 'Here is Miss Nickleby . . . wondering why the deuce somebody doesn't make love to her' (p. 238). Bets are laid by the spectators on her willingness to deny this, until distress overcomes her:

> The poor girl, who was so overwhelmed with confusion that she scarcely knew what she did, had determined to remain perfectly quiet;

but fearing that by doing so she might seem to countenance Sir Mulberry's boast, which had been uttered with great coarseness and vulgarity of manner, raised her eyes, and looked him in the face. There was something so odious, so insolent, so repulsive in the look which met her, that, without the power to stammer forth a syllable, she rose and hurried from the room. (pp. 239–40)

Such a commentary underlines the doubly voyeuristic structure of the narrative: one male deploring to the (?male) reader the details of a scene, which he describes at length, in which another male displays to an all-male audience what he can reduce a woman to by implicit sexual threat. In the episode which follows, where Hawk, alone with Kate, attempts to seize her, the same hypocritical viewpoint is maintained by the narrator alone. And so with all such scenes. For the pattern of female innocence beset by the sexual threat which is 'most alien' to it is found recurrently throughout Dickens' novels at all periods. The intensity of the threat and the degree of elaboration vary, but similar episodes are found involving Emma Haredale and Dolly Varden and the rioters, Mary Graham and Pecksniff, Agnes Wickfield and Uriah Heep, Pet Meagles and Rigaud, Lizzie Hexam and Bradley Headstone. Echoes are found in Louisa Gradgrind's dealings with Bounderby, Esther Summerson's with Jarndyce and Amy Dorrit's with John Chivery. The last example, John Jasper's sexual persecution of Rosa Bud, shows skilfully a painful extreme of terror. He has only to look at her as she sings and plays in public for her to become paralysed with fear. As she tells Helena Landless later:

'He has made a slave of me with his looks. He has forced me to understand him, without his saying a word. . . . When I sing he never moves his eyes from my lips. When he corrects me, and strikes a note . . . he himself is in the sounds, whispering that he pursues me as a lover . . . tonight when he watched my lips so closely as I was singing, besides feeling terrified I felt ashamed and passionately hurt. It was as if he kissed me.' (*Edwin Drood*, pp. 53-4)

At least two other episodes show her terrorised in the same way. But despite the repetitious lingering over the menace, Jasper was presumably to have been thwarted as were Quilp, Hawk, Pecksniff, Heep, Headstone (as well as Rigaud and Chivery) before him.

Two structural characteristics of these narratives have now become clear. First, they describe a pattern of menace moving innocence/ignorance to confusion and increasing terror but never beyond it to knowledge. The potential for menace depends on the characteristics described in the first section of this chapter, the so-called 'idealising' of nubile girls. Second, these sequences involve varying degrees of voyeurism constituting a male exchange of represented females: a male narrator presents male power over a terrified woman to a male audience, a situation sometimes raised to higher power by the presence of a manipulating figure like Hawk. This structure is familiar to those who analyse pornography in the real world:

> The pornographer is the speaking 'I' of pornographic representation, and he may or may not represent himself as the subject/master in the scenario of the picture. He is in direct communication with another subject, the spectator or reader. . . . In the picture or out of it, he objectifies the woman/victim for the reader, the viewing subject who contemplates the object. If the pornographic scenario represents the male master–subject, the woman object is twice objectified: once as the object of the action in the scenario, and once as the object of the representation, the object of viewing. The former objectification is optional, the latter is always present: it is a structural feature of pornographic representation. (Kappeler 1986: 52)

Under cover of a representation of nubile girls frequently dismissed as merely sentimental, Dickens in fact evolved a narrative syntax that created a ghost pornography which emphasised strikingly the fact that the only role for a nubile girl in any version of these syntactic structures is irretrievably that of sexual object. Agency is impossible for her, and her 'idealising' merely turns her into a vehicle for this verbal exploitation.

It is consequently all the more striking that one central narrative, read paratactically, appears to draw attention to the nature of such structures. For in *Great Expectations* gender roles are transposed in a similar series of episodes to create bewildering effects. It is a beautiful and nubile girl, Estella (carefully not described at all except in general terms), who menaces and torments a young man through her power to attract him sexually. Her pander or presenter is another woman and the purpose of their joint enterprise is to inflict as much suffering as possible. Estella acts ambiguously enough to suggest that she herself is attracted, though for her the whole process is a charade. Only the underlying structure remains the same as those described above, and as a result the motivating cruelty is illuminated. For even one man to find himself in Pip's position (as object) is extraordinary in Dickens. Again, as elsewhere in his texts, a rare variation on his norm shows at least a degree of linguistic contradiction not usually recognised. It is typical of the way in which spasmodically a recognition occurs, in ludic form, of the undesirable implications that underlie his own sexist representations.

Chapter 3

Fallen girls

Fallen girls and their significance

The sign in Dickens' language closest to that of the nubile girl in the semantic field of gender is one usually regarded as its antithesis, *the fallen woman*. In a sense, as will be seen later, the assumption is valid. The adjective, perhaps the most succinct of narratives in its description of an irresistible progression downwards, is used for Harriet Carker's perception of Alice Marwood as her 'fallen sister' (*Dombey and Son*, p. 462). The alternative term *lost*, more erasure than description, also common in the literature of the period, is applied to herself by Martha Endell in *David Copperfield*: 'I am bad, I am lost' (p. 582). It tends, however, to be preferred mainly by those like Dinah Mulock Craik (1858), who in the chapter of her *A Woman's Thoughts About Women* called 'Lost women' is concerned to urge compassion for women who have sinned sexually:

> No one can have taken any interest in the working-classes without being aware how frightfully common among them is what they term 'a misfortune' . . . [and] the women who thus fall are by no means the worst of their station. I have heard it affirmed by more than one lady . . . that many of them are . . . refined, intelligent, truthful and affectionate. (1858: 289–91)

This overt pleading is not found in Dickens and I have therefore chosen the first of the two adjectives, in combination with the noun *girl*, since it draws attention to an important fact: what Nancy in *Oliver*

Twist (1839), Alice Marwood in *Dombey and Son* (1848), Martha Endell and Emily in *David Copperfield* (1850) have fallen from is girlhood as described in the previous chapter. It is as ruins and wrecks of girls like Rose Maylie that, to an extent, they see themselves or are seen by others. The zealous Brownlow tells Nancy, counterpointing her against his angelic Rose: 'The past has been a dreary waste with you, of youthful energies mis-spent, and such priceless treasures lavished, as the Creator bestows but once and never grants again' (*Oliver Twist*, p. 315). Martha Endell transforms the natural imagery used of Dora Spenlow and her like when she compares herself to a once pure river:

> 'I know that it's the natural company of such as I am! It comes from country places, where there was once no harm in it – and it creeps through the dismal streets, defiled and miserable – and it goes away, like my life, to a great sea, that is always troubled.' (*David Copperfield*, p. 581)

The prostitute that Redlaw meets in 'The haunted man' is presented by the narrator in similar terms as the natural thing that is already blighted. She is 'one whose bloom and promise were all swept away, as if the haggard winter should unnaturally kill the spring' (*Christmas Books*, p. 365). Harriet Carker reads past girlhood into the degraded figure of Alice Marwood, James Carker's ex-mistress, whose name is itself a negation of the natural:

> She thought of all that was perverted and debased within her, no less than without: of modest graces of the mind, hardened and steeled, like these attractions of the person; of the many gifts of the Creator flung to the winds like the wild hair; of all the beautiful ruin upon which the storm was beating and the night was coming. (*Dombey and Son*, p. 462)

These are quite evidently the ruined girls, antithetical to nubile ones.

Structurally, the broad meaning of the ruined girls is also made clear by a series of firm contrasts with the unruined girls. Nancy makes the comparison of herself with Rose Maylie when urged to leave the brutal Sikes:

> 'When ladies as young, and good and beautiful as you are . . . give away your hearts, love will carry you all lengths – even such as you, who have home, friends, other admirers, everything to fill them. When such as I, who have no certain roof but the coffin-lid, and no friend in sickness or death but the hospital nurse, set our rotten hearts on any

man, and let him fill the place that has been a blank through all our wretched lives, who can hope to cure us?' (*Oliver Twist*, pp. 274–5)

Martha, when she lies with disordered hair, weeping at the feet of the still innocent Emily, makes the contrast pictorially. Even Annie Strong, the very young wife of an elderly husband, a mere ghost of a fallen girl, who apparently falls into the arms of her lascivious cousin, Jack Maldon, makes, for a time, a contrast with the unfallen, virtuous Agnes Wickfield. Copperfield, watching Agnes' father watching her and Annie, senses that 'Mr. Wickfield seemed to dislike the intimacy between her and Agnes, and to watch it with uneasiness':

> And now, I must confess, the recollection of what I had seen on that night when Mr. Maldon went away, first began to return upon me with a meaning it had never had, and to trouble me. The innocent beauty of her face was not as innocent to me as it had been; I mistrusted the natural grace and charm of her manner; and when I looked at Agnes by her side, and thought how good and true Agnes was, suspicions arose within me that it was an ill-assorted friendship. (*David Copperfield*, p. 240)

Fallen, by pointing to this recurrent contrast/difference, captures an essential emphasis in Dickens' handling of the group. The term *girl* has the advantage that, as well as relating back to its use as part of the sign dealt with in chapter 2, it serves to indicate a relationship of contrast with the second term of a sign to be discussed later, *the passionate woman*. The latter will be used in chapter 6 for those whose fall or putative fall occurs in the context of marriage. Both these signs obviously belong in the same area (deviancy) of the semantic field under discussion.

At the time when Dickens wrote, female deviancy of a sexual kind was subsumed into accounts of prostitution. As Hemyng was to put it later, 'literally every woman who yields to her passions and loses her virtue is a prostitute' (in Mayhew 1861–2: 215). Certainly, seduced and deserted girls were assumed to have taken the first step across the frontier into what was perceived as a vast and threatening territory. As Walkowitz makes clear in her *Prostitution and Victorian Society* (1980), a 'public outpouring of concern' about the 'Great Social Evil' (p. 32) manifested itself in the 1840s. Her aim is to analyse and produce as accurate a picture as possible of the historical facts about the social class of prostitutes, the reasons for their way of life, the period of its duration and the social and economic structures which surrounded it. It is clear also, however, that there is a traditional coding which represents and contains the threat that large-scale prostitution represented. This coding might be called 'literary', though it is to be found in pictorial art, as Nead has shown in her impressive study, *Myths of Sexuality* (1988). It was not confined to 'fictional' forms but can be found throughout the period up to the 1860s, at least in the more informally structured social surveys like Mayhew's. It is the individual reworking of this language by Dickens that I wish to address.

By the 1840s this linguistic code was already being contested in public discussions. In its early stages the attack focused, particularly for charitable motives, on modifying the significance of fallen women, traditionally seen only as agents of evil and in no sense as victims. As W. R. Greg wrote in the famous article, 'Prostitution', in the *Westminster Review* in 1850: 'we feel called upon to protest against the manner in which prostitutes are almost universally regarded, spoken of and treated. . . . No language is too savage for these wretched women . . . outcasts, Pariahs, lepers' (p. 450). This points to the central mechanism of the language in question: its use of biblical and religious register. As Walkowitz says, Greg took the pose of 'a charitable realist hoping to retrieve prostitutes from their outcast status' (p. 43).

Radical attempts to rewrite the language used to describe prostitution were made by those who, wishing to accept the status quo, were intent on turning it into an unemotive subject for regulation. This attempt crystallises in its clearest form in William Acton's *Prostitution Considered in its Moral, Social and Sanitary Aspects in London and other Large Cities; with Proposals for the Mitigation and Prevention of its Attendant Evil* (first published 1857; rev. 1870). The clinical-sounding title itself is a linguistic challenge to the earlier kind of semi-religious title such as *Magdalenism: An inquiry into the extent, causes and consequences of prostitution in Edinburgh* by William Tait (1840). Against this background of linguistic flux one can place this aspect of Dickens' novelistic idiolect in order to question the assumption that he produced a series of perfect stereotypes of the fallen woman. The 'literary' myth was very persistent in novels until late in the century but, like Elizabeth Gaskell's *Ruth*, Dickens' texts involving fallen women are affected by the contemporary debate. At least an unconsidered use of the code was now impossible; shifts of various kinds and recodings were likely.

In order to bring out the changes that Dickens effected, it is necessary briefly to describe the traditional significance attaching to the fallen woman during the early part of his career. The traditional meaning depended, as the religious register suggests, upon an equation between female sexual transgression and damnation that links it back to Eve and the first Fall. This coding represented those who had fallen, like the fallen angels, as a 'multitudinous amazonian army the devil keeps in constant field service for his own ends' (Miller 1859: 5). The pious Christian attempt to modify this can be illustrated by Dinah Mulock Craik's overwriting of this old idea of damnation with the more intelligent traditional version of damnation as wilful loss of God. The prostitute can then be seen to be carrying an evil burden from which 'no kindness . . . no concealment of shame, or even restoration of good repute, can entirely free her' (Craik 1858: 297). By transforming corruption into self-torment Craik opens the way to pity and possible charitable intervention that cannot possibly interfere with divine retribution.

Even Acton occasionally appropriates the religious register of those he is attacking to cast himself in the role of Good Samaritan to the anti-regulators' Levite and Pharisee. Typically, however, his challenge takes the form of contradictory assertion as unsubtle as a health warning. He needed to dismantle first of all the antithetical signs Mary/Eve, Virgin/Whore (in Dickens' terms nubile girl/fallen girl) in which the negative defines the positive: 'It is no more a necessary consequence that the loss of her honour should divest one woman of the other feminine attributes than that another who has preserved it should be in all other respects perfect and complete' (Acton 1857: 4). This strikes at the heart of the signifying system but does not immediately change it. It operates on a different discursive level from the code itself, while novelists like Dickens were already working on the same level where metaphor, metonymy and other rhetorical devices were constantly used.

Dickens' first work, *Sketches by Boz* (1836), uses the traditional language in virtually unchanged forms. There are several prostitutes presented as the antithesis of nubile girls: in terms of physical appearances that can be conventionally read off to reveal what is better called nature than character. 'The pawn-broker's shop' portrays 'a young female whose attire, miserably poor but extremely gaudy, plainly bespeaks her station. The rich satin gown with its faded trimmings, the worn-out thin shoes, and pink silk stockings, the summer bonnet in winter, and the sunken face . . . cannot be mistaken' (*Sketches by Boz*, p. 194). This is far from Dora and her garden-hat but the linguistic method is the same; the inventory, blending clothes with physical characteristics, and the use of the definite article for the possessive serve to create an image like that of the nubile girl in that it is unspecific, and hence iterable. Indeed, the iterability of the figure of the prostitute was evidently recognised at the time. A casual allusion by Dickens to 'the female in the faded feathers' in 'Gin shops' was enough to evoke it (*Sketches by Boz*, p. 185). It was sketched in derisively by Acton, only to be dismissed with a flat contradiction: 'It is a little absurd to tell us that "the dirty, intoxicated slattern in tawdry finery and an inch thick in paint", long a conventional symbol of prostitution, is a correct figure in the middle of the nineteenth century' (Acton 1857: 53). Such physical descriptions are at first glossed by Dickens as symbols of degradation and corruption: the elder sister in 'The prisoners' van' merely shows that two extra years 'of additional depravity had fixed their brand upon . . . [her] features as legibly as if a red-hot iron had seared them' (*Sketches by Boz*, p. 273). A similar depravity is seen in the young prostitute visiting her procuress mother in Newgate (*Sketches by Boz*, pp. 205ff.).

Even in the novels there are residual traces of the original convention, since fallen women there tend to tawdry finery. A description first applied to Nancy and later transferred to the substitutable Bet combines 'red gown, green boots' and 'yellow curl-papers' (*Oliver Twist*, p. 79). Both girls are dishevelled and heavily painted. But, significantly, the descriptions of Martha Endell and Alice Marwood shift the emphasis of such accounts to the poor and inadequate nature of their clothing, muting its tawdriness and suggesting pathetic vulnerability to the elements. Martha is 'flaunting' in her style of dress but 'too lightly dressed' for the weather (*David Copperfield*, p. 277). With Alice the finery disappears and is replaced by colourless and inadequate clothes:

> the soil of many country roads . . . clotted on her grey cloak . . . no bonnet on her head, nothing to defend her rich black hair from the rain, but a torn handkerchief; with the fluttering ends of which, and with her hair, the wind blinded her, so that she often stopped to push them back. (*Dombey and Son*, p. 462)

Already the meaning attached to such figures has lost some of its horror.

It is clear that the women in *Sketches by Boz* are no more physically or sexually realised than their merely nubile sisters. In the novels, however, there is a change. The necessary sexual accessibility is skilfully signalled by a single feature: the undressed or loosened hair to which the implication of undressing generally could be attached, as it could also to any other suggestion of being *déshabillée*. No grown-up middle-class girl would deliberately appear in public with her hair streaming over her shoulders. To do so is to suggest intimacy and to break down the barriers between the private and the public. There is a flouting of convention and respectability in appearing before mere acquaintances in this way. The near-madness of Estella's witch-like mother is plainly indicated by the fact that she serves at Jagger's table with 'streaming' hair (*Great Expectations*, p. 201). Nancy, whose hair is normally merely bundled up untidily, shows the extent of her drunken misery to Fagin by 'lying with her head upon the table, and her hair straggling over it' (*Oliver Twist*, p. 166). Sexuality is thus economically troped without 'offensive' physical reference.

But this use of loosened hair for the fallen women in the novels carries another significance that is not attached to the prostitutes in *Sketches by Boz*. It indicates an allusion to the Gospel figure of Mary Magdalen, the repentant prostitute who dried Christ's feet with her hair. Consequently, it signals repentance, or some degree of it, as is confirmed by its pictorial appearance on the shoulders of conscience-stricken or drowned women such as Nead (1988) illustrates. More of that meaning is brought out in the episode where Martha is glimpsed by Copperfield after her confessional scene with Emily. He sees her sitting on the ground: 'I saw but little of the girl's face over which her hair fell loose and scattered, as if she had been disordering it with her own hands' (*David Copperfield*, p. 288). Most strikingly, loose disordered hair is central to the representation of Alice Marwood. Her bitter awareness of what it means allows her to turn it into a way of resisting her grievance against her seducer, James Carker; and of expressing distaste for her own wantonness by touching, pulling or even biting it. At one point, for instance, she holds it up roughly 'as if she would have torn it out; then, threw it down again, and flung it back as though it were a heap of serpents' (*Dombey and Son*, p. 464).

Fallen girls in the novels are not, of course, mere penitents but are charged with other unexpected meanings. Nancy, the first to appear in a novel, seems at first close to her fallen sisters in *Sketches by Boz*, with her disordered appearance and her 'perfume of Geneva'. She is not obviously distinguished from a stereotypical group encountered by Fagin in a public house, who attract attention by their repulsiveness.

Some have 'the last lingering tinge of their early freshness almost
fading as you looked', others have 'every mark and stamp of their sex
utterly beaten out' presenting 'one loathsome blank of profligacy and
crime' (*Oliver Twist*, p. 164). Moreover, Nancy willingly undertakes
the recapture of Oliver after he has escaped from Fagin's gang. And
yet eventually she reveals characteristics proper to the womanly
woman, from whom she is patently dissociated by dress, manners,
speech. She preserves a commitment to Sikes paralleling the loyalty
expected of even a wronged wife till death, 'I am drawn back to him
through every suffering and ill-usage and should be, I believe, if I
knew that I was to die by his hand at last' (p. 274). This is reminiscent
of the attitude Ellis urges on the wronged wife whose husband has
taken a mistress. Whatever her sufferings, she must maintain an
unwavering dutifulness, not forgetting that having 'no other than a
legal claim . . . she is . . . a low, lost thing, more lonely, pitiable and
degraded than the veriest outcast from society who still retains a hold
upon her husband's love' (Ellis 1843a: 203).

More striking than this shadowing of a wife's role is Nancy's
conversion to womanly compassion when she comes to feel Oliver's
innocence and vulnerability. This is still described in terms of an
unwomanly 'passion of rage' potentiated by 'recklessness and despair' (p. 103), traditional enough words to apply to a prostitute but
here relating to the passionate rages of an unexpected and long-
sustained womanly virtue. The rewriting of her as not totally evil,
while still using these familiar terms, eases the transition obviously
felt by the narrator to be a difficult one. He attempts to theorise it in a
confused passage before Nancy's interview with Rose Maylie about
the plan to save Oliver. He starts with a bold assertion that her life
'had been squandered in the streets, and among the most noisome of
the stews and dens of London, but there was something of the
woman's original nature left in her still'. But he soon modifies this by
a reference to her evil and contradictory pride, since 'even this
degraded being felt too proud to betray a feeble gleam of the womanly
feeling which she thought a weakness' (p. 270).

Equally contradictory are the meanings attached to the figure of
Martha Endell. She is a prime example of Dickens' exploitation of the
fallen girl in the old style as an expression of moral, social and
physical degradation and contamination. This is fully evoked in
a much-quoted passage in which Martha stands, contemplating
suicide, on the bank of the Thames. Her subsequent comparison of

herself to the river turns the narratorial description of it into a representation of her. Like the wrecks of machinery that surround it, she represents human debris 'vainly trying to hide itself'. She is the vessel that receives human pollution as the river does from 'sundry fiery works' from which pour 'heavy and unbroken smoke'. She stands for a contagion that is more than symbolic, the plague of disease:

> Slimy gaps and causeways, winding among old wooden piles, with a sickly substance clinging to the latter, like green hair, and the rags of last year's handbills offering rewards for drowned men fluttering above high-water mark, led down through the ooze and slush to the ebb-tide. There was a story that one of the pits dug for the dead in the time of the Great Plague was hereabout; and a blighting influence seemed to have proceeded from it over the whole place. Or else it looked as if it had gradually decomposed into that nightmare condition, out of the overflowings of the polluted stream. (*David Copperfield*, p. 580)

The narrator supports Martha's own identification of herself, for she appears to him as 'a part of the refuse it had cast out, and left to corruption and decay' (*ibid.*).

Yet it is Martha, moved by the plight of Emily after her seduction by Steerforth, who devotes herself to the 'woman's mission' of saving one of the fallen. This is a task that Craik urges upon 'our honourable women, mothers and matrons' (Craik 1858: 309); and that Miller approves in 'a few benevolent ladies' who, out of compassion 'have nobly exerted themselves to reclaim their fallen sisters', behaviour, he assures them, entirely compatible with 'womanly-modesty' and 'lady-like propriety' (Miller 1859: 36). Ironically, in this instance the sisterhood between Emily and the prostitute Martha is closer than that of gender alone.

Unlike Nancy, who is always spotlighted, Martha moves from her prominence in the long description on the river bank to the invisibility of Little Dorrit when she becomes a womanly Samaritan. It is only through Mr Peggotty's telling of the story that the reader learns briefly of her rescue of Emily from the brothel: 'When my child stood upon the brink of more than I can say or think on – Martha . . . saved her'. The semi-religious language that he uses fleetingly transforms the Magdalen into a Christ figure: 'She come, white and hurried, upon Em'ly in her sleep. She says to her, "Rise up from worse than death, and come with me!" . . . and brought her safe out . . . from that black pit of ruin!' (*David Copperfield*, p. 623). Like the opulent picture of her as corrupt and contagious, this is strongly iconographic; retrospectively, it conflicts with and destabilises her earlier significance.

But this conflict of meaning attaching to Nancy and Martha undermines the dichotomy between the two signs of Virgin and Whore/nubile girl and fallen girl, which is central to a whole system of signification that is frequently used to contain anxieties relating to class as well as gender (Nead 1988: 94). Prostitutes are typically presented as lower class, and fallen women become declassed. As Walkowitz shows, prostitutes *were* predominantly from the lower classes of society; but there is an interesting divergence between the facts as she presents them and the significance attached to them in the 'literary' language. The reasons for prostitution, as Walkowitz shows in some detail, are largely economic: it was the 'best of a series of unattractive alternatives' (1980: 31). The correlation with working-class females, however, was traditionally interpreted as a manifestation of depravity of the masses. As late as 1862 Hemyng was arguing that 'To be unchaste amongst the lower classes is not always a subject of reproach . . . the depravity of manners . . . begins so very early, that they think it rather a distinction than otherwise to be unprincipled' (Mayhew 1861–2: 221).

The practice of turning the working classes into a scapegoat by making them the ultimate sources of crime and vice was by the mid-nineteenth century virtually automatic. Even Hemyng in the midst of his statistics reverts to traditional language to delimit this vice of prostitution in terms of gender and class. Disregarding the clients, he is necessarily left with the women themselves and he is determined to make clear that they have no middle-class connections. He invokes the biblical notion of 'bad seed' to lend authority to a somewhat confused statement:

> It is difficult to say what position in life the parents of these women were in, but generally their standing in society has been inferior. Principles of lax morality were early inculcated, and the seed that has been sown has not been slow to bear its proper fruit. (Mayhew 1861–2: 217)

He dismisses claims to a higher class:

> Loose women generally throw a veil over their early life, and you seldom, if ever, meet with a woman who is not either a seduced

governess or a clergyman's daughter; not that there is a word of truth in the allegation – but it is their peculiar whim to say so. (Mayhew 1861–2: 217)

It is also true, as Walkowitz points out, that many prostitutes' clients, even the majority, were from the lower classes. This still left a good many middle-class men frequenting them also, but this fact is not given prominence. The traditionalist Miller's 'remedies', for instance, all relate to 'the masses': they must be elevated by education, deterred from excessive alcohol, prevented from being 'vicious and idle parents', and made to wear less provocative clothes (Miller 1859: 14ff.). When middle-class females momentarily surface in the wrong territory as 'ladies of intrigue' (married women who take lovers and unmarried women who gratify their passion secretly), Hemyng hastily gets rid of them in a passage that ties together female virtue, middle-class status and English nationality:

> This sort of clandestine prostitution is not so common in England as in France and other parts of the Continent, where chastity and faithfulness among married women are remarkable for their absence rather than their presence. As this vice is by no means common or a national characteristic . . . it can only expect a cursory notice at our hands. (Mayhew 1861–2: 258)

Acton's apparently innovative strategy is to break down the barrier separating middle-class virtue from working-class vice: the vice is not so bad, not so extensive, not so deeply engrained, not so threatening. All that is needed are the proper sanitary regulations to control things perfectly well. His method of argument is to deploy the contemporary practice of categorising and grading different types of fallen women for the verbal construction of an alternative social hierarchy of 'shades of . . . prostitution . . . as numberless as those of society at large' (1857: 53). He elaborates on the prostitute as not always unrefined, ill-dressed, poor, undernourished or syphilitic. His admirer, Greenwood, grasped the point of this strategy and made it. The two territories were not entirely separate but linked; there was a legitimate frontier post: 'It is for the interest of society at large, as well as for that of the guilty individual, that we should never break down the bridge behind such a sinner as the miserable "unfortunate" even' (Greenwood 1869: 331). Regulation would facilitate this passage of the guilty woman back to respectability across the bridge.

Dickens, as has been shown, had moved towards a romantic

version of Acton's central tenet that it is not 'a necessary consequence that the loss of honour should divest a woman of the other feminine attributes' (1857: 4). He had explored the scope for added pathos, dignity and nostalgia which resulted if gleams of characteristically feminine goodness shone sadly from the human ruins of girlhood such as Nancy and Martha. But this striking change in one part of the traditional coding of female sexual transgressors brought him into collision with another as yet unmodified part. There was by the 1830s a clear convention, in relation to the speech of characters in novels, requiring that those 'of dignity and moral worth' speak 'a language fit for heroes to speak', free of lower-class markers (Page 1973: 97). This accounts for the middle-class speech of Oliver Twist, brought up in a brutalising workhouse but representing the principle of Good, and happily accommodated finally among the Maylies. The convention is not to be taken as implying that all users of middle-class forms of speech are morally worthy; but the more limited implication it carries (that those of moral worth must use them) maintains the connection between a specific class and specific moral values.

The flaws inherent in such a novelistic convention are revealed whenever Dickens is making the point that virtue is independent of social status – in female characters like Lizzie Hexam. They also surface in the figure of Nancy precisely because she represents the two conflicting versions of the prostitute. Initially, since she is the female representative of the 'dregs of life', a 'pupil' of Fagin, a streetwalker and a thief, she shares the language of Sikes and Fagin. When these two press her early on to recapture Oliver she is reluctant on pruden- tial grounds. Her refusal is uttered in their own language: 'it won't do; so it's no use a-trying it on, Fagin' (*Oliver Twist*, p. 79). When Sikes urges her, saying that she is not known locally and would not be recognised by anyone, her reply is equally colloquial: 'And as I don't want 'em to, neither, it's rather more no than yes with me, Bill' (p. 79). Her rare early utterances are sprinkled with thieves' cant, the mark of the criminal insider: 'The young brat's been ill and confined to the crib' (p. 95). With her adoption of womanly, middle-class compassion Dickens comes up against the problem of how to make her speak a language fit for heroines, or at least for a (partly) virtuous woman. Like the related problem with Lizzie Hexam described in chapter 1, this one is dealt with by modifications of her speech away from its originally tainted type. Her first defence of Oliver is still slightly coloured by forms like *'em* and *aye*. Gradually, as she grows more voluble about her views on the cruelty of Sikes and Fagin towards the boy, the lower-class markers become fewer. And by the time of her encounters with Rose Maylie she is as articulate and as middle-class in her speech as her auditor:

> 'I am the infamous creature you have heard of, that lives among the thieves, and that never from the first moment I can recollect my eyes and senses opening on London streets have known any better life, or kinder words than they have given me, so help me God! Do not mind shrinking openly from me, lady. I am younger than you would think to look at me, but I am well used to it. The poorest women fall back, as I make my way along the crowded pavement.' (*Oliver Twist*, p. 271)

This would be the middle-class moral assessment of Nancy and must therefore be dissociated from the group she belongs to, which is lower class and immoral. Paradoxically, she must now speak of herself in a speech free of 'vulgar' markers and characterised by a middle-class control of syntax. The gradual changes made in the form of her language serve to reveal the illogicalities in the convention relating to speech in the novel and in doing so draw attention to the ideological subterfuge on which it is based.

Later there is at least one instance in a novel in which Dickens questions the basis on which this linguistic convention is constructed. He does so without making the connection and in a characteristically paratactic fashion. The comment arises out of the apparently contrasting figures of Edith Dombey and Alice Marwood, the wife and ex-mistress of a Carker brother respectively. The two meet when Alice is peddling goods for a living in the country and Edith perceives the other woman as a distorted reflection of herself. When she asks 'What is it that you have to sell?' Alice, who is given to bold descriptions of her own degradation, replies: '"Only this," . . . holding out her wares, without looking at them. "I sold myself long ago"' (*Dombey and Son*, p. 553).

The fallen girl's words are a striking echo of Edith's earlier frank assertions to her mother the night before Dombey's proposal:

> 'You know he has bought me . . . or that he will tomorrow. He has considered of his bargain . . . he thinks it will suit him, and may be had sufficiently cheap. . . . There is no slave in a market; there is no horse in a fair: so shown and offered and examined and paraded . . . as I have been for ten shameful years.' (*Dombey and Son*, pp. 381–2)

Reformers and regulators linked society to the alternative world of
prostitution by a bridge across which a fallen woman could travel
back; Dickens here links the two by showing supposedly lower-class
vice distinguishable at the centre of middle-class society, when he
compares its marriage market to prostitution. And he does so not
through the figure of a wicked Becky Sharp, but through the beautiful
and high-minded Edith, whose spontaneous reaction to her own sale
shows a womanly delicacy of sensibility. The point is stressed by the
narrator after a scene between Alice Marwood, her procuress mother,
Mrs Brown, and Harriet Carker:

> Were this miserable mother, and this miserable daughter, only the
> reduction to their lowest grade, of certain social vices sometimes
> prevailing higher up? In this round world of many circles within
> circles, do we make a weary journey from the high grade to the low, to
> find at last that they lie close together, that the two extremes touch, and
> that our journey's end is but our starting place? Allowing for great
> difference of stuff and texture, was the pattern of this woof repeated
> among gentle blood at all?
>
> Say, Edith Dombey! And Cleopatra, best of mothers, let us have
> your testimony! (*Dombey and Son*, p. 477)

If the implications of the answers to these questions had been
developed they would have been destructive of the whole equation of
sexual purity with the middle-classes and vice with the lower ranks.
They would make a mockery of its manifestations in the convention of
a language fit for hero(ine)s. For the passage is a powerful reworking
of the use that traditional accounts make of sexual transgression as
damnation. It evokes the Dantean moral world of circles within
circles, though the progress perceived is in the reverse direction from
La divina commedia, not from hell to heaven but from heaven to hell.
And by a bitter irony this journey itself is finally revealed to be
another circle linking 'low' back to 'high', the nether world to the
upper. Hypocrisy adds an extra dimension to the great social evil
when it is found amongst the upper classes. All this remains an insight
that Dickens does not sustain and it indicates yet once more how
powerfully his imagination worked in forbidden areas revealing the
gaps, contradictions and illogicalities in the linguistic code which he
overtly supported.

Narrative syntax: the harlot's progress

As there is a traditional significance attaching to the prostitute, there is also a traditional story to reinforce it. Speaking of what she calls 'the Mythology of the Life and Death of the Prostitute', Nead says that the myth took the form of 'a sequence of fall, decline and death' (1988: 140). One such narrative, occurring in a semi-anecdotal form in Hemyng, will serve as an example of many:

> A woman who has fallen like a star from heaven, may flash like a meteor in a lower sphere, but only with a transitory splendour. In time her orbit contracts, and the improvidence that has been her leading characteristic through life now trebles and quadruples the misery she experiences. To drown reflection she rushes to the gin palace, and there completes the work that she had already commenced so inauspiciously. The passion for dress, that distinguished her in common with her sex in former days, subsides into a craving for meretricious tawdry, and the bloom of health is superseded by ruinous and poisonous French compounds and destructive cosmetics. A hospital surgeon gave us the following description of the death of a French *lorette* . . . (Mayhew 1861–2: 214)

Such a fall through the circles of hell to death is reworked in a wide range of writing, both 'literary' and 'non-literary'. Dickens himself used it in his 'Appeal to fallen women', printed in late 1847, urging them to read how terrible it was

> to grow old in such a way of life, . . . – to escape an early death from terrible disease, or your own maddened hand, and arrive at old age in such a course – will be an aggravation of every misery that you know now. . . . Imagine . . . the bed on which you, then an object terrible to look at, will lie down to die. (*Pilgrim Letters*, 5, p. 698)

Acton naturally needed to transform the narrative as well as the significance attaching to the sign of the fallen woman. Just as he argued that sexual transgression did not necessarily corrupt the whole woman, similarly he tried to subordinate the story to the individual. The lives of the women in question were, he claimed, larger than this. Deviancy could be merely an isolated episode, some kind of subplot in the main story of a woman's whole life: 'I repeat that prostitution is a transitory state, through which an untold number of British women are ever on their passage' (Acton 1857: 73).

This claim reverses the traditional narrative pattern (characteristic of Dickens' own narrative patterns generally) in which a course is already determined regardless of the individual, where events have primacy over intention. In this tradition woman is still grammatically the subject who falls, declines and dies; but logically she is not the agent of her own destiny. She is seduced or misled into a fall and after that is sucked into a downward vortex. She finally undergoes a death which characteristically falls upon her like the weather, usually in the form of a physical and psychological collapse. The various versions of a harlot's progress deny a woman agency as surely as that other much-favoured sequence in which she is a pseudo-agent who 'chooses' a husband but who can 'choose' only from the two or three who have first chosen her.

What is noticeable in Dickens' treatment of the standard story is, surprisingly, the emergence of some degree of autonomy in the fallen and hence sexualised girls, such as the nubile girls, always the object of menace, never attain. This development of agency is not progress-ive over time, rather the reverse: there is a little shown in *David Copperfield* (1850), more in *Dombey and Son* (1848) and a great deal in *Oliver Twist* (1839). This achronology reflects, as I shall show, how his representations are repeatedly destabilised by contradictory elements from their very beginning.

The first source from which the idea of the fallen woman acting as agent in her own story arises is that of atoning. I have suggested that the sequence of fall–decline–death can be read as a social ritual of atonement with the woman as its scapegoat object. But within such narratives a move towards agency occurs when the third stage itself is expanded into 'the fallen woman atones' by her actions. This is what happens in Gaskell's *Ruth* (1853) when in the central story Ruth brings about her own death by nursing fever victims. She has acted as the catalyst for her particular form of death, which provides closure for the whole novel.

Similarly, atonement involving a degree of agency also occurs with Martha Endell in *David Copperfield*. She has no central role to play in Copperfield's life but in the Emily–Steerforth subplot she does have a part. It is precisely on account of her fallen status that Copperfield selects her to find Emily, lost in the London underworld, though he finds it difficult to name the fallen woman to Mr Peggotty: 'If she should come here . . . I believe there is one person, here, more likely to discover her than any other in the world. Do you remember – bear what I say, with fortitude – think of your great object! – do you remember Martha?' (p. 577). Her acceptance of the task is only indirectly reported and is strongly religious in tone. Coming as it does immediately after the scene imaging her contagion and despair by the river, it takes on the force of a religious vow, the fulfilment of which will bring about a degree of reparation and possible purification:

> If she were not true to it, might the object she now had in life, which bound her to something devoid of evil, in its passing away from her, leave her more forlorn and more despairing, if that were possible, than she had been upon the river's brink . . . and then might all help, human and Divine, renounce her evermore! (p. 584)

She finds Emily, effects her return to Mr Peggotty and so resolves the Emily–Steerforth affair, which can be erased by Emily's emigration to Australia with her adoptive father.

Though this is merely a subplot, and though Martha's control of events is small, it is significant that what she does relates to something outside her own predicament. She sees it as an act of atonement but it is different from the generalised nursing activities of Gaskell's Ruth, undertaken as a gratuitous act of atonement extraneous to the plot (replaceable by many alternatives) and resulting in her death. The total passivity of Emily, whose life, by contrast, can be summed up as a string of past participles – seduced, rescued, redeemed, removed – underlines Martha's active role. In fact, Martha seems to serve as a surrogate, acting out a more extreme version of Emily's fall and so preserving her from carrying the full significance of the fallen woman.

Alice Marwood, like Martha, remains a conventionally marginalised figure but manages to affect the course of events even in the main plot relating to Edith Dombey's elopement with Carker. Her intervention springs directly out of her bitterness towards Carker, on account of his seduction and desertion of her. In an act of revenge she effects a meeting between Dombey and Rob the Grinder at which the latter reveals that the destination of Edith's and Carker's flight is Dijon. This sets Dombey off on a pursuit which results eventually in Carker's death under the wheels of a train. As with Martha's activities, Alice's active role is minimally described, a method familiar in traditional figures like the fallen Esther in Gaskell's *Mary Barton* (1848). But none the less, what Alice does is crucial to the main narrative and it is not undone by her subsequent repentance and attempt to reverse its effects by warning Harriet, Carker's sister, of his danger. The revelation she brings about remains pivotal to the plot and she is, though invisibly, its agent.

But it is above all Nancy, the first prostitute in the novels, who sustains a central place in the main plot and effectively determines its course in a way which suggests the appropriateness of the title 'Sikes and Nancy' that Dickens chose for the famous reading version of the novel with which he became so obsessed. In the struggle between the forces of good and evil for Oliver himself it is she who, unknown at first to the other thieves, liaises with the middle-class forces of good and virtually brings about the identification of the boy and his preservation from the evil intended by his wicked brother, Monks. Her actions, though depending on knowledge that she has acquired because of her criminal connections, alter the direction of a sequence of events unconnected with her fallen state. She is more autonomous, more active and more continuously an agent than any other fallen or nubile girl. Power, or at least a degree of power, is thus returned, ironically not to the womanly woman but to the outcast who is normally inscribed only in the underplots and margins of the text. Such a change also diminishes the emphasis usually reserved in the traditional story for the event which stands for both peripety and closure: the harlot's death. The death remains important but not uniquely so.

The consummation of the sexual transgressor's decline in death seems to have been largely accepted by religious writers, by many medical conservatives and those few novelists such as Gaskell who risked handling the subject at this time. Its narrative cohesion, based on a familiar pattern in which retribution follows transgression, lent it religious authority. Nead believes that ending the story with a self-caused death in the form of physical decline or suicide by drowning was a means of relieving respectable society of responsibility or guilt for what happened to the fallen woman (Nead 1988: 139). But it has surely another significance: the woman's erasure is society's painless reparative sacrifice for its own sexual transgression. The link with the Christian ideas of Fall and Atonement is made clearly by the religious associations of the language used to describe the woman's end. Charlotte Bronte turns naturally to such language when asking of the eponymous heroine of Gaskell's *Ruth* 'Why should she die?' She concludes to the author:

And yet you must follow the impulse of your own inspiration. If *that* commands the slaying of the victim, no bystander has a right to put out his hand to stay the sacrificial knife; but I hold you a stern priestess in these matters. (in Shorter 1908: 2. 264)

Bronte of course is here equivocating with the word 'victim'. Overtly, Ruth is the victim of literary inspiration; covertly, she is the victim of society, which requires that the wages of sin should be death.

Superficially at least Bronte accepts the need for a sacrifice; but even Acton, who challenges it bluntly, argues much of his case in biblical terms, setting himself up as the Good Samaritan to the prostitute over against the Levites and Pharisees of conservatism. And he alludes directly to the religious interpretation that he wishes to deny: the claim that 'Disease is a punishment for sin', or 'syphilis the penalty paid . . . for fornication' (Acton 1857: 9).

Presumably, death by drowning was written in as the appropriate form of suicide partly because it represented a process of cleansing. Certainly, it was the death preferred pictorially. Dickens both uses and evades this option simultaneously, making it ghost the real end of Nancy and Martha. Nancy predicts it for herself when Rose Maylie cries despairingly 'What can be the end of this poor creature's life?':

> Look before you, lady. Look at that dark water. How many times do you read of such as I who spring into the tide, and leave no living thing, to care for, or bewail them. It may be years hence, or it may be only months, but I shall come to that at last. (*Oliver Twist*, p. 316)

She is, in the event, wide of the mark: drowning is the subjunctive plot overlaid by the actual or indicative one of murder. Similarly, the traditional suicide is evoked as a prospect for Martha, who actually tries to throw herself into the river. Then it is deleted as she is prevented by Copperfield's physical force and Mr Peggotty's moral power:

> [she] struggled with me with such strength that I doubt if I could have held her alone. But a stronger hand than mine was laid upon her; and when she raised her frightened eyes and saw whose it was, she made but one more effort, and dropped down between us. (*David Copperfield*, pp. 580–1)

Again she appears to stand for Emily as well as herself and to shadow suicide and escape from it for her too. But significantly, she does not have to die for Emily but merely to go to the brink for her, an interesting use of subjunctive (or negative) plot that is paralleled, as I shall show later, in Dickens' treatment of adultery.

Alice Marwood, on the other hand, does not, despite her development of a certain autonomy, evade the statutory death in the form of non-specific disease. This variant had already developed several potential meanings. Originally and continuingly, it was an embodiment of the idea that 'The wages of sin is death.' However, as social writers' attempts to refute the idea by statistics reveal, it was also interpreted as meaning that the wage for this particular sin was venereal disease. In more compassionate or more squeamish accounts it bears a strange resemblance to the mysterious decline of girls like Nell Trent and is passed off as a kind of release, or at least comfort. And in the telling of an ingenious writer like Hemyng it could combine the last two interpretations. Syphilis, he says, is more usually fatal in innocent girls than in hardened prostitutes. The girls

> whose devotion has not yet bereft them of their innate modesty and sense of shame, will allow their systems to be so shocked, and the constitutions so impaired, before the aid of the surgeon is sought for, that when he does arrive his assistance is almost useless. (Mayhew 1861–2: 213)

Thus the death of a prostitute from these causes could be made to bear one or more different emphases.

Undoubtedly, the emphasis that Dickens chooses to give it in *Dombey and Son* is the innocuously nebulous one. Alice goes into some kind of decline between chapters 53 and 58 until after 'many months' she has become pale and weak (p. 822) and returned to religion. She has a 'weak frame' but 'strong' eyes (p. 782) (referred to elsewhere as 'lustrous') presumably suggesting the serenity and satisfaction with which she faces death. Harriet leaves her and

> The lustrous eyes, yet fixed upon her face, closed for a moment, then opened. . . . The same eyes followed her to the door; and in their light, and on the tranquil face, there was a smile when it was closed. They never turned away . . . life passed from her face, like light removed. (p. 786)

The ease of this transition echoes the smooth death of Nell Trent (which is not even described in its actual moment). If life has become a 'light' to be extinguished this is not the same death as the mere cutting off of degradation: the end of the harlot's progress has been subtly changed.

Martha's erasure is an equally final but more humane variation on death – emigration – to which both Greg (1850), Miller (1859) and Greenwood (1869) allude, and which Dickens in practice encouraged in collaboration with Angela Burdett-Coutts. More daringly, he allowed Martha to acquire a husband in Australia, though only on the exigent terms that he is a man living in a remote place who needs a housekeeper and sexual partner, and that, as Mr Peggotty says 'Wives is very scarce theer' (*David Copperfield*, p. 744).

Nancy, through her actual death, however, becomes Dickens' Tess. She dies, but not in any of the traditional ways. Despite her prediction that she will end like most of her sort in the river, she also realises that a return to Sikes may mean her death: 'I am drawn back to him through every suffering and ill-usage and should be . . . if I knew that I was to die by his hand at last' (p. 274). The escape route that Martha takes, or perhaps a more comfortable one, is offered to Nancy by Rose Maylie and Mr Brownlow. As this declaration shows, she rejects it, and in doing so exerts the same autonomy that she has shown in the defence of Oliver. Like Tess, she is exercising an option when she chooses death. Perhaps all that their choice amounts to is a choice of *how* they will die. But by choosing the path that ends in her murder by Sikes, Nancy invokes a death that sweeps away the traditional significance of the death of a prostitute as cleansing, restitution, divine justice, merciful oblivion. She remains unambiguously a victim. The brutal death she undergoes fundamentally alters the apparently ineluctable force of the harlot's progress, putting traditional meanings in question. All this is at the beginning of Dickens' career as a novelist and was never repeated, but it serves to indicate the subtext that always develops when a woman falls and so becomes sexualised: a kind of agency accompanies the changes.

Elsewhere in Dickens, however, stranger exponents of the fallen-girl sign are to be found in two women who at first are not recognisably fallen at all, but each of whom, as Acton claims of many, 'amalgamates with the population' (1857: vi): Rosa Dartle in *David Copperfield* as a genteel, middle-class companion to her relative Mrs Steerforth; and Miss Wade in *Little Dorrit* as an independent woman of means. Rosa turns out to have been willingly seduced by James Steerforth and Miss Wade by Henry Gowan (subsequently Pet Meagles' husband). Neither has needed to rehabilitate herself under the cloak of marriage, nor do they do so. Their respectable status is clearly established in the text before their earlier transgressions come to light, when the women themselves reveal them willingly and unnecessarily.

As with other fallen women their physical appearance is prominent. It is marked by a significant darkness that contrasts with the angelic fairness of nubile girls, and which they share with Alice Marwood. Each in her way, however, is, as the narrator says of Rosa, 'remarkable'. Rosa literally bears Steerforth's imprint in the form of a scar running downwards across her mouth that he inflicted on her with a hammer in childhood (p. 252). This is the physical index of her passionate nature and changes its colour with her fluctuating emotions. Miss Wade (who, significantly, has no more familiar name) is marked by the satanic quality of her dark beauty:

> The shadow in which she sat, falling like a gloomy veil across her forehead, accorded very well with the character of her beauty. One could hardly see the face, so still and scornful, set off by the arched dark eyebrows, and the folds of dark hair, without wondering what its expression would be if a change came over it. . . . Although not an open face, there was no pretence in it. I am self-contained and self-reliant; your opinion is nothing to me; I have no interest in you, care nothing for you, and see and hear you with indifference – this it said plainly. (*Little Dorrit*, p. 23)

What they share with other fallen women in Dickens' novels is that they both feel that there is something terribly wrong with them, though it only superficially resembles the sense of degradation that preoccupies Martha Endell and Alice Marwood. They evince the passionate despair that usually characterises the prostitute but it is transformed with each of them into something specific to their individual natures. They have meaning as individuals as well as stereotypes. With Rosa the despair takes the form of a fierce frustration at the loss of Steerforth as her lover: 'As his fancy died out, I would no more have tried to strengthen any power I had, than I would have married him on his being forced to take me for his wife. We fell away from one another without a word' (*David Copperfield*, p. 686). With Miss Wade the traditional rage appears as an angry perception of herself as someone repeatedly scorned because of her illegitimate birth. Gowan's rejection was one more example for her of what she had long felt to be her destiny. With both of these women, then, the idea of the female transgressor as an outcast takes on a different significance. The question of their moral status is subordinated in their self-image to individual considerations: they are emotionally, not morally, alienated.

Neither plays a significant role in the main plots of the novels in which they appear, though Miss Wade makes an abortive attempt to abduct Pet Meagles' maid Tattycoram (alias Harriet Beadle) in order to turn her into another 'self-tormentor'. By the control of their public fate, however, the two women may be said to achieve a degree of agency, since they avoid the familiar path downwards. Rosa's seduction is partly re-enacted when Steerforth draws her out for Copperfield's benefit trying 'with his utmost skill to charm this singular creature' into being a pleasing companion.

> That he should succeed, was no matter of surprise to me. That she should struggle against the fascinating influence of his delightful art . . . did not surprise me either. . . . I saw her features and her manner slowly change; I saw her look at him with growing admiration; I saw her try, more and more faintly, but always angrily . . . to resist the captivating power that he possessed; and finally, I saw her sharp glance soften. (*David Copperfield*, p. 371)

This displaced seduction is itself ambiguous, since Copperfield's involvement allows it to be read as Steerforth's seduction of him. The revelation that Rosa and Miss Wade have sinned has no effect on their subsequent social status and it is clear from the time which has elapsed since they did so that it has not precipitated the usual decline and death. Subsequently, Rosa returns to her ambivalent relationship with Steerforth's mother, Miss Wade remains an eccentric but respectable woman. The accounts of their sexual sinning are so brief and unelaborate that it is possible for the reader to overlook them altogether. They are women whose falls have been swallowed up in the wider passions of their lives. They both achieve striking individuality and that in itself is enough to make them a violent contrast with many other homogenised figures of women in Dickens' novels. The text allows them to 'integrate' with the rest of the world which does not even notice what their story has been, nor that it is subversively at odds with the official story of the harlot's progress. Surreptitiously Dickens once again privileges the fallen girl over her unfallen sister as he makes a degree of agency the concomitant to identity as a sexual being: the subtext thus asserts that to deny sexuality to women (such as nubile girls) is a way of denying them agency.

Chapter 4

Excessive females

Female voices and their significance

It might be expected that the implied fate of nubile girls, that predicted by the name, would be the norm, and that their budding promise would flower into marriage. Ellis does see the qualities required of girls as necessary for a successful transition to wifehood: they are needed not 'merely to give zest to conversation' or to 'throw an intellectual charm over the society of the drawing-room' but in order to make 'the happy individual' who possesses them into a perfect wife and companion for her husband (Ellis 1843a: 114). But of all the nubile girls in Dickens' novels only three marry much before the end of the narratives in which they appear: Dora Spenlow (Mrs David Copperfield), Lucie Manette (Madame St Evrémonde/ Darnay) in *A Tale of Two Cities* and Bella Wilfer (Mrs John Harmon/ Rokesmith) in *Our Mutual Friend*. And in these three instances the representation of a married girl is inhibited by the usual significance of such girls, as described in chapter 2, with its insistence on physical immaturity and on the etherealness of the angel. Since part of that significance appears to block off a transition to knowledge in both carnal and intellectual senses, the language of representation continues after marriage to be that described earlier but now, as will be shown, at odds with their new marital state.

A comparison that may be kept in mind at this point is the one that can be made with lower-class wives (never former nubile girls), who appear as simple providers and who are, in terms of the domestic economy, themselves basic provisions: good housekeepers, good plain cooks, efficient nursing mothers and resilient and resourceful help-mates. It would be contrary to the decorative and passive nature of nubile girls to be transposed into Polly Toodles, Mrs Bagnets or Mrs Plornishes. Nevertheless, the three girls mentioned all marry and become pregnant some time before the end of the narratives in which they appear. Lucie Manette's marriage takes place earlier in the story than those of the other two when, in chapter 18 of *A Tale of Two Cities*, she marries the Marquis St Evrémonde under his assumed name of Charles Darnay. Her role in the text is entirely passive, and the dramatic incidents in which she is involved are dealt with by surrog-ates such as Mr Lorry and Miss Pross, as well as Carton and others. Her function is to act as an emotional barometer for the fluctuating fortunes of her father and, more particularly, her husband, when they are caught up in the bloody events of the French Revolution. She is there (complete quite soon with female child) to enhance the pathos when St Evrémonde is under sentence of death, and to focus the relief when his release is effected by Sydney Carton's brave self-sacrifice in taking his place under the guillotine.

The account of her earlier years of marriage, compressed into a few paragraphs at the beginning of chapter 21, illustrates the difficulties of translating an angel into a housewife and nursemaid. Household duties have to be encoded into the language used in the previous representation of the three women as nubile girls. They are, in Lucie's case, metonymically troped by the act of spinning a suitably 'golden thread' which binds 'her husband, and her father, and herself, and her old directress and companion, in a life of quiet bliss'. This equation of Lucie with Penelope, the wife of Ulysses, raises the domestic to the level of myth: daily routine is meretriciously replaced by the poignancy of a wait for a long-absent husband as she passes her time 'in the tranquilly resounding corner, listening to the echoing footsteps of the years' (*A Tale of Two Cities*, p. 200).

Similarly, her embarrassing pregnancy is displaced onto an (imaginary) mortal illness, shrouding it also in the pathos fitting a Penelope:

> For, there was something coming in the echoes, something light, afar off, and scarcely audible yet, that stirred her heart too much. Fluttering hopes and doubts – hope, of a love as yet unknown to her: doubts of her remaining upon earth, to enjoy that new delight – divided her breast. (p. 200)

The domestic environment is rewritten as echoes and waves, features nebulous enough to surround an angel; and the picture of a husband, grieving over the early grave that she never in fact experiences, seems to replace childbirth as the culmination of her wait/gestation. Ambiguous 'waiting', then, figures pathos not pregnancy:

> Among the echoes then, there would arise the sound of footsteps at her own early grave; and thoughts of the husband who would be left so desolate, and who would mourn for her so much, swelled to her eyes, and broke like waves.
>
> That time past, and her little Lucie lay on her bosom. (p. 200)

She continues 'ever busily winding the golden thread . . . weaving the service of her happy influence through the tissue of all their lives', while the infant Lucie can soon be translated into 'a sacred joy' (p. 200). From this point on, with the sexual issue safely negotiated, Lucie is required only to weep or rejoice.

A similar linguistic problem is presented by Bella Wilfer's marriage, although it takes place at a relatively later point in *Our Mutual Friend*. By her verbal independence, at least, Bella has previously deviated from the ideal represented by Lucie and the rest, as when she complains of old Harmon's will that left her to John Harmon 'like a dozen of spoons, with everything cut and dried beforehand, like orange chips', and asserts 'I love money, and want money – want it dreadfully' (p. 37). When she is redeemed from these minor sins by a submissive acceptance of penniless John Rokesmith (alias rich John Harmon) there is an attempt to represent her as a domesticated angel. In this instance the contradiction proves linguistically intractable. At first, the usual evasive displacement is attempted by presenting the necessary housekeeping as a parlour game in which she participates with an uncharacteristic earnestness, rendered inappropriate by the narrator's heavy-handed irony:

> John gone to business and Bella returned home, the dress would be lain aside, trim little wrappers and aprons would be substituted, and Bella, putting back her hair with both hands, as if she were making the most business-like arrangements for going dramatically distracted, would enter on the household affairs of the day. Such weighing and mixing and chopping and grating, such dusting and washing and polishing, such snipping and weeding and trowelling . . . such making and mending . . . and above all such severe study! For Mrs. J.R., who had never been wont to do too much at home as Miss B.W., was under the

constant necessity of referring ... to a sage volume entitled The
Complete British Family Housewife. (*Our Mutual Friend*, pp. 681–2)

This turns her role as housewife into a mere vehicle for the display of
charmingly kittenish ineffectiveness. Such a coding is abandoned to
give way to the language of fairy-tale as Rokesmith/Harmon reveals
his princely wealth by surprising her with 'a dainty house', more
suitable than their cramped quarters for an angel, complete with
aviary, tropical birds and fishes and a fountain. It is 'tastefully
beautiful' already and has a bedroom furnished with no more
substantial articles than 'an exquisite toilette table', holding an ivory
casket of jewels, as well as a nursery 'garnished as with rainbows'
(p. 778). These adjuncts, intended to restore her to nubile girlhood,
merely draw attention to the gap between the earlier Bella and this
one.

Bella's announcement that she has conceived takes the form of a
declaration to her husband that a ship is 'upon the ocean ... bringing
... to you and me ... a little baby (p. 688). The same displacement of
physiological fact onto a platitudinous reference to a ship coming
home is sustained when the months of gestation are referred to
as winds and tides rising and falling 'a certain number of times'.
Childbirth itself becomes 'the ship upon the ocean' making its voyage
safely and bringing 'baby Bella home' (p. 755) and Bella, before this,
presumably in order to cut her down to fit the uneasy language, is
happy to be referred to as John's 'little wife'.

This unease comes across as an attempt by the narrator to sustain
a monocular vision faced with the paradox of an asexual and purely
decorative girl who, unfortunately, marries. In *David Copperfield* the
paradox is resolved for the narrating Copperfield because the game-
playing child-wife is now differently perceived. Dora was seen at first
as the ideal nubile girl, the tastiest dish of all and, as I have pointed
out, Copperfield eats her. But he then has to live with her as partner,
housekeeper–cook and prospective mother of his child. She evidently
fails in all three roles despite his premarital attempts to instruct
her by giving her a prettily bound cookery book (which only makes
her head ache), and by trying to initiate her into discretion over
joints of meat (which only makes her pout her mouth into a girlish
bud). Not unexpectedly, the child-like nubile girl turns into Copperfield's 'child-wife', who cannot even provide an adequate dinner for
his undemanding friend Traddles, cannot manage her 'immense'

account-book nor share his troubles. When he is overwhelmed by work and anxiety he keeps them to himself 'for my child-wife's sake':

> Thus it was that I took upon myself the toils and cares of our life, and had no partner in them. We lived much as before, in reference to our scrambling household arrangements; but I had got used to those, and Dora I was pleased to see was seldom vexed now. (*David Copperfield*, p. 552)

Again the difficulty of presenting a pregnant angel manifests itself and is overcome by describing the pregnancy not as an event but as a dispositional weakness: 'as that year wore on, Dora *was not strong*' (my emphasis). Miscarriage is displaced onto the removal of the hope that 'a baby smile might change my child-wife to a woman', as the foetus 'fluttered for a moment on the threshhold of its little prison, and . . . took wing' (p. 596). As Dora herself recognises, her failure as a wife is the result of her essential irrationality and irresponsibility, which cannot be changed. Copperfield himself only sees that he cannot change her, not that her childish qualities were the cause of his infatuation in the first place. Expectations of expert housewifery never appeared in his delight in her appearance and antics with Jip; and yet he feels himself to be a man gravely disappointed in a legitimate hope:

> What I missed, I still regarded – I always regarded – as something that had been a dream of my youthful fancy; that was incapable of realisation; that I was now discovering to be so, with some natural pain, as all men did. (*David Copperfield*, p. 595)

What Copperfield is discovering here is something which conflicts with, for instance, Slater's assertion that for Dickens ' "womanliness" . . . was not a matter of nurture but of nature, something timeless and universal' (Slater 1983: 302). Many of the more familiar contemporary statements of the womanly ideal were in fact couched in the language of exhortation. In perhaps the most famous, 'Of Queens' Gardens' (1865), Ruskin repeatedly defines not merely 'a wife' but 'a *true* wife' along with 'the woman's *true* place and power' (my italics); using repeatedly verbs of obligation (*should, must, ought to*); and endowing the whole piece with an illocutionary force that is plainly directive. More detailed works such as Ellis' are precise recommendations on how to turn yourself into the perfect or 'true' wife, mother or daughter, a task requiring sustained and meticulous effort. Ellis' coerciveness is more direct and the 'gentle reader' is asked to bear in mind, at one point,

> that in speaking both of the characteristics and the influence of a certain class of females, strict reference has been maintained, throughout the four preceding chapters, to such as may be denominated *true* English women. (Ellis 1839: 118)

. Slater and others assume that those who espouse the womanly ideal do so by creating a sign perfectly matching it – the ideal woman, straight from the hand of the creator. But 'the ideal' is rather to be seen as the theology/ideology underlying the whole semantic field relating to 'womanhood'. In modern representations, whether visual or verbal, a physically unattractive spinster is given a negative significance relating to the idea of women as primarily sexual objects just as directly as the positive meaning attaching to metonymic 'blondes'. Similarly, whereas nubile girls do represent a variation on the paragons proffered as blueprints by Ellis and Ruskin, the married women so often satirised in Dickens' novels are equally clearly linked to the ideal, but in a negative way. Further, they offer a reconsideration of the idea of woman's nature captured in the nubile girls. Their significance will now be described in detail to show how it subverts that of the opposing sign dealt with in chapter 2.

The reiteration of the phrase 'true woman' and the repeated application of the adjective to the ideal generally imply a desirable norm to be aimed at, achievable by a conscientious struggle for conformity, and not something women are born to. True, in a period that usually took an essentialist view of the nature of women in respect of character and temperament as well as physiology, certain qualities were thought to be inherently theirs. But, as the comments of Ellis and Ruskin show, such qualities did not in themselves constitute womanly perfection: they became so only when rightly balanced and directed by a proper understanding of their complementary function.

Dora thus reveals to a marked extent the feminine lack of masculine rationality; but with her it appears in excess, unconstrained by regulatory judgement or judicious training (such as the mothers of England were meant to provide). Copperfield's attempt to bring restraint to bear comes too late, so that the intuitive, instinctive/capricious, wilful behaviour so attractive to the male admirer in the drawing room strikes him as disastrous once he has authorised it to be let loose in other areas of his household. Nubile girls have been (and continue to be) represented by Dickens on the unthinking assumption that innocent virtue is a natural concomitant to extremely youthful beauty: in them nature and nurture are equated. But when, in Dora, such a girl follows her assumed destiny into marriage she reveals that Dickens has failed in such figures to come to grips with the fact that his own concept of 'womanliness' is based not just on a belief in inherent female qualities but also in the belief that they need to be curbed in order to reach it.

When he does face this fact in the representation of women who enter novels already middle-aged and married, he reveals a conviction that even middle-class females seldom achieve the ideal, and that the consequences of their not doing so are both grotesque and disruptive. With such women the problem of how to handle the transition from nubile girl to wife does not arise. With the exception of Flora Finching and Mrs Skewton, there is no hint that they have ever been nubile girls anyway. But they indicate the need for a radical reappraisal of what the nubile girl is supposed by Slater to stand for: female nature in its primitive state. My interpretation is that the narrator's satirical representation of them is an attempt to contain the rampant femaleness that they are seen to embody. There are, of course, a few women, usually unmarried, who, like Sally Brass in *The Old Curiosity Shop* or Miss Murdstone in *David Copperfield*, are shown to be grotesque through their appropriation of male characteristics. Sally Brass is said to resemble her brother physically, and is derided for her skill in the masculine role of lawyer's clerk. Significantly, in both these aspects she is sarcastically referred to as strikingly 'feminine' to make the point that 'a male female is repulsive' (1861 interview cited by Slater 1983: 316). However, more threatening, and therefore more in need of containment than Sally Brass and Miss Murdstone, who can be written off as freaks of nature, are those who are unwomanly not because they are endowed with masculine qualities but because they have female qualities in unregulated and disruptive excess. \d Mrs Joe – Seen as excessive fem

Such individuals show that the womanly ideal is based on a misogynistic view of what women are really like if left to nature without nurture. What they are like is illustrated not by nubile girls, but by Mrs Nickleby, Mrs Varden, Mrs Gamp, Mrs Skewton, Mrs Joe Gargery, Mrs Jellyby, Mrs Pardiggle, Flora Finching, Mrs Wilfer and others. In them characteristics that in prescriptive works appear in a form flattering to woman (as a result of the regulation and civilising of inherent qualities) are seen as quite negative. It is for this reason that such married women are grouped under the sign *excessive female(s)*: the qualities in question are assumed to be biologically grounded – hence the noun chosen; and they are here presented in their natural state as potentially threatening as well as comic – hence the adjective.

In the representation of these middle-aged and married women, appearance and food, so prominent in manifesting the significance of nubile girls, play only minor roles. Often they are absent altogether. Sometimes they are briefly mentioned, as when Esther notices, with Mrs Jellyby, that she wears a dress that 'didn't really meet up at the back, and that the open space was railed across like a lattice-work of stay-lace' (*Bleak House*, p. 37). This symbol of her chaotic domestic economy and her physical excess is reinforced by her disastrous way with food: 'We had a fine cod-fish, a piece of roast beef, a dish of cutlets, and a pudding; an excellent dinner, if it had had any cooking to speak of, but it was almost raw' (p. 40). Mrs Jellyby is femaleness in its raw or uncooked state, a figure which makes it clear that Dickens has failed to recognise the contradiction in his own account of edible girls as luscious to the palate although in their natural state: womanliness is as much the result of civilising cooking as roast goose, delicious steak, pudding and lumps of turkish delight.

However, the area of life in which Mrs Jellyby and similar women express their natures is one recognised by Ellis as more important even than 'personal services, handwork, and domestic management' – the conversational arena: 'I am inclined to think that a married woman, possessing all these, and even beauty too, yet wanting conversation, might become "weary stale, flat, and unprofitable" in the estimation of her husband' (Ellis 1839: 121). More than this, she sees it as the proper way for them to exert influence:

> Women have the choice of many means of bringing their principles into exercise, and of obtaining influence, both in their own domestic sphere, and in society at large. Amongst the most important of these is *conversation*; an engine so powerful ... that beauty fades before it ... and wealth in comparison is but as leaden coin. (Ellis 1839: 119)

Nor is Ellis unique in her preoccupation with women's language; like food, the subject occurs regularly in both positive and negative ways in the accounts of those who represent women. Emancipated women, for instance, are often seen as likely to engage in shocking talk, in articles such as that in the *North British Review* in 1850 on 'The social position of woman': 'Her conversation often owes not a little of its piquancy to an undercurrent of allusion, which would shock and humiliate an unenlightened woman, if she understood it' (p. 528). Conversation is referred to almost as often as food in Nightingale's 'Cassandra', though she sees the kind of conversation that Ellis recommends as an instrument of oppression matching enforced meals. Men, she tells the reader, say to their wives 'Why don't you talk in society?' (in Stark 1979: 42), expecting them to produce a little but not too much conversation. Wives must suppress their female desire to babble and must allow no-one 'to be too much absorbed in, or too long about, a conversation' (p. 33). Nightingale rebels against such restraints: 'I can pursue a connected conversation, or I can be silent; but to drop a remark, as it is called, every two minutes, how wearisome it is!' (in Stark 1979: 42). As with food, where she can dream of 'spiritual' sustenance, she presents the only alternative to such talk as fantasy: a 'phantom companion' for 'every thought' with whom women like herself could hold long imaginary conversations on 'that which interests them most' (p. 26). She chafes at restraints such as Ellis urges, and ridicules the prevailing and ambiguous belief that if 'man and woman approach any of the high questions of social, political or religious life, they are said to be going "too far"' (p. 28).

Conversation, then, is frequently seen as women's sphere and a testing ground for their progress towards the ideal. Ellis has many recommendations to make about it, always on the assumption that, left to themselves, women produce undesirable kinds of talk. The practitioners of the latter take many shapes, to which she devotes two chapters of condemnation in *Women*, where she berates the professional conversationalists, the hobby-horse riders, the users of jargon, the self-obsessed, the compulsive anecdotalists, the unstoppably garrulous, the malicious gossips and those who talk at random. It is significant that when routinely she praises silence or near silence as the ultimate perfection, she reveals her misogynistic belief that it is *naturally* difficult for women and 'proverbially synonymous with a degree of merit almost too great to be believed in as a fact' (1839: 145). Women can only achieve perfection as conversationalists (with all that perfection stands for) by proper adaptation. Underlying all Ellis' recommendations is an account that links them to the idea of achieving the 'true' woman's complementary role by self-restraint:

> There could be no agreeable conversation carried on, if there were no
> good listeners; and from her position in society, it is the peculiar
> province of a woman, rather to lead others out into animated and
> intelligent communication, than to be intent upon making communi-
> cations from the resources of her own mind. (Ellis, 1839: 145)

This translates the view of women as secondary into a linguistic
model in which they are there to respond, to enable and to withhold
the fruits of an inferior intelligence. Married women, therefore, can
appropriately be defined in terms of their voices: of how they live up
to the linguistic ideal. Such a preoccupation with speech chimes
perfectly with Dickens' obsession with every aspect of how individuals speak, from voice quality to syntax. It also follows naturally
from narrative sequences in which, typically, agency is denied to
women since it is virtually the only form of self-expression left.

What, then, is thought to constitute the femaleness that creates
women's voices? The most commonly accepted basis for describing it
seems to be the assumed dichotomy between men as rational and
women (in complementary fashion) as intuitive, a view which is often
directly linked to biology. As an article in 1824 on 'Men and women:
brief hypothesis concerning the difference in their genius' puts it: 'All
the education in the world will never produce a woman as *strong* as the
strongest man, either in mind *or* body . . . *equal* in bodily or intellectual
power' (*Blackwood's Edinburgh Magazine*, 1824, p. 389). This deficiency
of intellect can take various forms. With Mrs Jellyby, for instance, it
manifests itself in the public orations in which she describes in public
language the public service that she has so unwisely allowed to
replace the private service that is her duty:

> 'You find me, my dears, as usual, very busy. The African project at
> present employs my whole time. It involves me in correspondence with
> public bodies, and with private individuals anxious for the welfare of
> their species all over the country. I am happy to say it is advancing. We
> hope by this time next year to have from a hundred and fifty to two
> hundred healthy families cultivating coffee and educating the natives
> of Borrioboola-Gha, on the left bank of the Niger.' (*Bleak House*, p. 37)

What has happened to her is that though her womanly compassion is
abundant it has been diverted through the bad judgement that results
from a limited intelligence into the wrong sphere for a married
woman. There she concerns herself, in a 'feminine' fashion, with
detail; but her concern should be reserved in her first place for the

comfort and happiness of her own dirty, suffering family, not scattered over one hundred to two hundred foreign families. Her pompously rhetorical way of speaking marks out this irrational deviation which she shares with Mrs Pardiggle.

But usually the female lack of intellectual power shows up in women's speech in more traditional ways. From at least the time of Shakespeare's Mistress Quickly onwards, garrulous inconsequentiality has been seen as the hallmark of women speaking. With Dickens it is the frequency of its occurrence and the extremes it reaches that are so striking. The lack of logic (and of syntactic control which enacts it) is familiar in many of Dickens' married women, such as Mrs Nickleby, Mrs Varden, Flora Finching, Mrs Gamp and others. A typical example is the first of these who, for instance, when discussing what Kate Nickleby is to wear at her uncle's infamous dinner-party even starts, as the narrator says, by flying off 'at an acute angle':

> 'Let me see . . . your black silk frock will be quite dress enough . . . with that pretty little scarf, and a plain band in your hair, and a pair of black silk stock – Dear, dear' cried Mrs. Nickleby, *flying off at another angle.* (*Nicholas Nickleby*, p. 230; my emphasis)

Added to this inconsequentiality (which is presumably what Ellis would have meant by 'talking at random') is Mrs Nickleby's total inability to rise above the particular to any form of general reasoning. And the narrator makes quite plain that the failure of her feeble attempts to achieve any generalisation other than cliché is a function of her unchecked femaleness:

> And to do Mrs. Nickleby justice, she never had lost – and to do married ladies as a body justice, they seldom do lose – any occasion of inculcating similar golden precepts, whose only blemish is, the slight degree of vagueness and uncertainty in which they are usually enveloped. (*Nicholas Nickleby*, p. 230)

Yet this traditionally misogynistic presentation of women's speech as characteristically an illogical gush, rendered comic by attempts at generalisation, is the main marker of the voices of married women in many of Dickens' novels.

Nor is a degree of incoherence the only defect in their speech: another recurring feature also depends on the intuition–reason dichotomy. It is described by the author of the 1824 article quoted above, who continues the passage cited as follows:

But then, the female will always be endowed with other properties, in a greater degree than the male. . . . Imagination, I believe, to be always in proportion to animal sensibility, and to the delicacy of animal organization; women, I believe, to have more animal sensibility, because they are more delicately organized than men; and therefore . . . women have *more* imagination than men. (*Blackwood's Edinburgh Magazine*, 1824, p. 389)

The writer goes on to use this attribution of extra imagination to women on biological grounds as an explanation of why they can produce fanciful works of literature but not treatises of a more profound kind. He is bent on giving different (but allegedly not inferior) women their (none the less) lesser due.

Dickens, however, takes the more negative view of women's propensity to be fanciful. Imagination – for him a concept more like our fancy – is shown to flourish in an unbridled form in women not schooled to complementarity. It is an excessive characteristic that expresses itself in riotous ways in their speech. One significant manifestation of it occurs when it causes women to create verbal fantasies with which they overwrite reality, creating small dramas within the 'real' ones of the wider text. As a result, several of his married women inhabit solipsistic worlds that they spin into being through their fanciful utterances in an attempt to impose them on others.

Some verbally create themselves as pathetic sufferers at the hands of husbands plainly shown to be deserving men. Mrs Nickleby, having induced her late husband to speculate with her dowry so as to lose it, revises the story to turn herself into its victim. This fiction to which she constantly returns subsequently is explicitly linked with gender, through a narratorial reference to married women of that untutored type to which she belongs: 'most married ladies, either during their coverture, or afterwards or at both periods' engage in such 'bitter recollections' (p. 26). Another such is Mrs Varden, who writes a similar script for herself while still a wife. Despite a sensible, affectionate and considerate husband, she takes this 'female' view of herself as 'persecuted perfection, and Mr. Varden, as the representative of mankind [as] . . . a creature of vicious and brutal habits, utterly insensible to the blessings he enjoyed' (*Barnaby Rudge*, p. 171). Though of a robust physique, she fantasises that as a result of her extreme sufferings at Varden's hands 'she would at some early period droop beneath her trials, and take an easy flight towards the stars' (p. 205).

Other comic wives or widows create similarly flattering scenarios for
themselves in which the element of excess is even more apparent: Mrs
Gamp, Mrs Gargery, Mrs Wilfer, who are all more vicious than Mrs
Nickleby and Mrs Varden, rewrite their domestic vices as persecuted
virtue. Mrs Joe Gargery, mediated through disenchanted male eyes,
sees herself as heroic in her domestic efficiency and magnanimous up-
bringing of her young brother. Her speech is ironically characterised
by its repeated reference to her bringing the orphaned Pip up 'by hand',
a phrase she evidently refers to the gentle nurture of a lamb that has lost
its mother, and he to her having a 'hard and heavy hand' that she frequently lays upon him and Joe. This picture of herself as long-suffering
is often bitterly reported by Pip in indirect speech in a way which suggests that her individual utterances are all obsessive repetitions of a
lunatic belief in her own goodness and Pip's total worthlessness.

Mrs Gamp's loquacity, on the other hand, is allowed to speak for
itself. Out of the reality that she is drunken, rapacious, greedy and
on occasion savagely cruel to her helpless patients, she devises an
identity for herself as compassionate, disinterested and abstemious.
This identity is evoked through her unstoppable and dislocated
anecdotes, usually supported by a reference to the witness to be borne
to their truth by the fictitious Mrs Harris:

> ' "Sairey Gamp," she says, "you raly do amaze me!" "Mrs. Harris," I
> says to her, "why so? Give it a name, I beg." "Telling the truth, then,
> ma'am," says Mrs. Harris, "and shaming him as shall be nameless
> betwixt you and me, never did I think, till I know'd you, as any woman
> could sick-nurse and monthly likeways, on the little that you takes to
> drink." ' (*Martin Chuzzlewit*, p. 405)

Another favourite role for female fancy to create has for the
narrator the added merit of relating to women's vanity as well. This is
the pose of romantic heroine in which a middle-aged woman, lacking
the requisite youth and beauty, vainly imagines herself the focus of
male admiration. Even Mrs Nickleby develops a subplot in which a
deranged neighbour who hurls suitably phallic cucumbers over her
garden wall is presented by her as a possible suitor and husband. She
reinterprets his 'smalls and grey worsted stockings' as the eccentricity
of 'a gentleman' proud of his legs, which are, no doubt, comparable to
the Prince Regent's (p. 481). But Mrs Nickleby has never been seen as
a nubile girl, unlike Flora Finching and Mrs Skewton, for whom some
traces of that state are evoked by the narrator in order to deride more

savagely their later aspirations which so grotesquely parody it. In the description of the middle-aged or elderly fantasies of these two women there is, by implication, a direct reappraisal of the surface perfection offered by the nubile girl who is assumed to be the product of untainted nature. Flora Finching (née Casby) is recalled by Arthur Clennam as a 'lily' of a girl with whom he was long ago in love but who, when he meets her again, has become an overblown 'peony': 'Flora, who had seemed enchanting in all she said and thought, was diffuse and silly' (*Little Dorrit*, p. 143). The 'fatal blow' to him, however, is that she wishes to take up her former identity and vainly tries to resurrect their old relationship, with the reluctant Arthur in the role of lover.

Her coercive invitations to him to participate in the old romantic drama flood out with an inconsequentiality and lack of syntactic control that exceed even Mrs Nickleby's and are accompanied by actions miming an extreme of affection and sensibility. Arthur, not surprisingly, is led to question his youthful assumptions about her, and to wonder whether, presumably because of her lily-like beauty, he then misinterpreted this gushingly idiotic female voice: 'Was it possible that Flora could have been such a chatterer in the days she referred to? Could there have been anything like her present disjointed volubility, in the fascinations that had captivated him?' (*Little Dorrit*, p. 144). Was the nubile girl as naturally perfect woman the figment of *his* imagination?

An even more elaborate reassessment of this sort underlies the presentation of Mrs Skewton in *Dombey and Son*, who shares with Mrs Gamp the claim to be the most excessive female among all Dickens' married women. Her youthful beauty is seen only dimly behind the role of Cleopatra (beautiful, full of sensibility and magnetic), which she claims for herself from her wheeled chair:

> The discrepancy between Mrs. Skewton's fresh enthusiasm of words and forlornly faded manner was hardly less observable than that between her age, which was about seventy, and her dress, which would have been youthful for twenty-seven. Her attitude in the wheeled chair (which she never varied) was one in which she had been taken in a barouche, some fifty years before, by a then fashionable artist who had appended to his published sketch the name of Cleopatra. . . . Mrs. Skewton was a beauty then, and bucks threw wine-glasses over their heads by dozens in her honour. . . . The beauty and the barouche had both passed away, but she still preserved the attitude. (*Dombey and Son*, pp. 283–4)

She also preserves the name, and both the narrator and Dombey's Mephistophelean crony, Bagstock, make ironic use of it. As a Cleopatra figure she adopts a languishing style of speech, full of overused adjectives (*charming, heavenly, sweetest, divinest, dearest, delightful*) such as Ellis castigates women for using (giving as an example the word *interesting*). At the same time a fault, later seen as attributable to senility, is made to seem like female inconsequentiality as she supplies gaps in her speech with fillers like *Whats-his-name, What-you-may-call-it* and *Thingummy*.

Furthermore, the attack on femaleness is covertly enforced by entwining her woman's language with a rapacity and ruthlessness that becomes 'female' by association. Under a smoke-screen of phrases praising 'Nature', 'the music of the heart' and 'gushing of the soul', she relentlessly bargains to effect the sale of her daughter, Edith Granger, to Dombey as his second wife. At Warwick Castle, where she hopes that Dombey will propose, the slippage between this speech and what goes on underneath is stressed, as she enthuses about 'those darling bygone times . . . with their delicious fortresses, and their dear old dungeons and their delightful places of torture . . . and everything that makes life truly charming!' The narrator laconically comments on the 'peculiarity' of this conversation with the watchful Carker: that 'with all their conversational endowments, they spoke somewhat distractedly, and at random' (*Dombey and Son*, p. 375). Logically, her cynicism has nothing to do with her gender but it speaks with the same voice and is therefore subsumed into it.

The dramas that these female voices enact all involve the contravention of Ellis' primary rule for womanly conversation: that women should act as fosterers, not as major participants who take a central part themselves. It is clear from her account of the many ways of offending against this rule that Ellis sees it as unnatural and difficult for women. And what Dickens similarly stresses is that these female voices naturally pervert what should be dialogue into monologue. What they produce is not for the well-run drawing room but, as the narrator underlines, for the theatre (the significance of which will be dealt with below. They are making a public spectacle of themselves by allowing their fantasies to run riot. This point is specifically made about Mrs Varden in one of the typically satiric commentaries that often accompany these fancifully egotistical female voices:

Indeed the worthy housewife was of such a capricious nature, that she not only attained a higher pitch of genius than Macbeth, in respect of her ability to be wise, amazed, temperate and furious, loyal and neutral in an instant, but would sometimes ring the changes backwards and forwards on all possible moods and flights in one short quarter of an hour; performing, as it were, a kind of triple bob major on the peal of instruments in the *female* belfry. (*Barnaby Rudge*, p. 54; my emphasis)

Reportage here viciously excises altogether the content of her speech, in order to stress its contrivance, emptiness and theatricality. When her sycophantic servant, Miggs, joins in to make this solo a 'duet', she expresses agreement by 'sniffs and coughs more significant than the longest oration' (p. 171). This reductive equation of the substance of the two women's speech with meaningless sounds parallels the culmination of satirical reference to public performance in a passage describing one of Mrs Gamp's addresses, elsewhere referred to as 'orations'. Hers becomes a virtuoso performance on a musical instrument, empty of logical content:

Mrs. Gamp was a lady of that happy temperament which can be ecstatic without any other stimulating cause than a general desire to establish a large and profitable connexion. She added daily so many strings to her bow, that she made a perfect harp of it; and upon that instrument she now began to perform an extemporaneous concerto. (*Martin Chuzzlewit*, p. 700)

The implications of the theatricality of female speech go beyond usurpation of the male role. Such a mode of speaking is multiply inappropriate: it is insubordinate in its claims for the self, indelicate in its clamour for public attention and, as perceived by these narrators, it is the outcome of false emotionalism. For such a complex of characteristics the *actress* was a suitable sign and that is what is alluded to here. Its usual significance is indicated by the tirade of the sexist figure of Conrad in Geraldine Jewsbury's strikingly advanced novel *The Half Sisters* (1848). He is speaking of the high-minded actress, Bianca:

'I never would marry an *artiste* of any grade. A woman who makes her mind public, or exhibits herself in any way . . . seems to me little better than a woman of a nameless class. . . . The stage is still worse [than writing] for that is publishing both mind and body too.' (Bk 2, 18–19)

Like food and speech this sign, alluded to negatively by Dickens, is rewritten positively by those challenging conventional views. These include Jewsbury in the novel referred to, which contrasts Bianca with her morally weaker half-sister, the womanly Alice, whom Conrad prefers. Florence Nightingale also speaks in 'Cassandra' of women 'when they are young' thinking that an actress's life is 'a happy one' (in Stark 1979: 41). Her argument seems to be that actresses are intellectual women rightly allowed to take a central role for which they purposefully prepared themselves.

The subordinate role allotted to women in conversation, which these strident and often histrionic female voices in Dickens' novels subvert, is emblematic of appropriate female behaviour in general. Women's intuition and sensibility are talents properly applied only when schooled to draw out and draw on other speakers; proper speech is metaphor for proper womanly conduct. The 'true' role of women is to influence, not to control those around them. But strident hysteria and self-dramatising are common enough in Dickens to show that, left to itself, the female capacity to influence is bent towards manipulativeness and domestic tyranny. The women discussed in this chapter have the most idiosyncratic forms of speech, but many other married women share some of their linguistic characteristics and threatening aspect. They include Mrs Weller, Mrs Sowerberry, Mrs Macstinger, Mrs Markleham, Mrs Snagsby, as well as others. It therefore seems permissible to describe the eccentric speakers as representative female voices.

Strikingly, rampant femaleness in Dickens cuts across class in a way that throws light on the question of whether in his work gender is transposed into social class or vice versa. Armstrong (1987), arguing for the latter view, sees gender in 'domestic fiction' as a way of concealing and containing class conflict. Discussing a broad category of 'monstrous women' (exemplified by Mrs Rochester in *Jane Eyre* or Nancy in *Oliver Twist*), she regards it as significant that, as she sees it, all have 'other than middle-class origins' (1987: 183). But this generalisation is not true of Dickens: in his novels femaleness in its natural state is disruptive and threatening in all classes. True, extreme examples like Mrs Gamp and Mrs Joe Gargery belong to the working class, and Mrs Varden, a locksmith's wife, to the lower-middle; but the social range of excessive females is wider than this. Mrs Nickleby, Flora Finching, Mrs Skewton, Mrs Jellyby and Mrs Wilfer are all middle class. And this wide social spread of the 'natural' as opposed to the 'true' woman is exaggerated by the absence of middle-class wives nurtured to proper womanly utterance and so to the perfect wifehood that is the assumed zenith of the feminine ideal. Many potential achievers of this state have, as critics have long since noticed, failed by prematurely and culpably dying from an excess of physical sensibility as Mrs Dombey, Clara Copperfield, Mrs Dorrit, Mrs Casby and Mrs Gradgrind do. Others, like Mrs Markleham (Anne Strong's mother in *David Copperfield*), Mrs Veneering and Mrs Pardiggle, are weak variants of the verbal tyrants described above, and offer no positive alternative to them.

In the working classes, as I have said, some successful wives emerge in the figures of Mrs Toodle, Mrs Bagnet, Mrs Rouncewell, Mrs Plornish and Mrs Boffin; but their success is of a simple kind, as providers of food and/or long-suffering affection. Their lack of middle-class refinement and its accompanying skills is underlined by a condescending and comic narratorial viewpoint. With the exception of Mrs Bagnet, a mouthpiece for common sense on her husband's behalf, they may be said not to have voices at all. They are certainly not embodiments of the ideal in its full perfection. By implication, disruptive femaleness transcends social class. The assumption makes clear that Dickens' hostile account of women's nature takes priority over class issues, a fact I shall revert to in chapter 6.

Slater regards these married women as the result of 'Dickens' extreme difficulty in reconciling the sexual with the domestic ideal' (Slater 1983: 311). But sexuality is not attributed to them any more than it is to nubile girls. If anything, it is the married state that is arbitrarily seen to be incompatible with the ideal for middle-class women.

Narrative syntax: the silencing of women

It is already evident that the plots attaching to these vociferous female voices in Dickens involve disruption to those around them; to some extent all the women described contribute to that disorder which constitutes for him the knitting-up of every plot. Naturally, their share of it is largely domestic. Mrs Jellyby is the prime example of an unwomanly female whose household inefficiency creates a pervasive chaos of bad food, inadequate heating, missing hot water, smoking chimneys and neglected children falling downstairs or getting their heads jammed between iron railings.

In another feminine sphere, that of the weekly nurse, Mrs Gamp
purveys not care and comfort but unkindness and discomfort to her
patients. When the fevered Lewsome tosses in delirium and cries out
for cooling water, her reaction is not to offer it: 'Sparkling water,
indeed! . . . I'll have a sparkling cup o'tea, I think. I wish you'd hold
your noise' (p. 413). Perversely, subversively, it is herself that she
cherishes, not her patient, with a warm fire, tea and buttered toast. In
doing so she illustrates a wrong relationship to food similar to that of
the gourmet Mrs Clennam, who also provides luxuriously for her
solitary self. A further perversion of womanly concern for others is
demonstrated later when the elderly Chuffey, agitated by a secret
knowledge of Jonas Chuzzlewit's misdeeds, begins to wander in
his mind. Mrs Gamp recommends professional interference with a
pitcher of cold water, and

> gave him some dozen or two of hearty shakes backward and forward in
> his chair; that exercise being considered by the disciples of the Prig
> school of nursing (who are very numerous among professional ladies)
> as exceedingly conducive to repose, and highly beneficial to the per-
> formance of the nervous functions. (*Martin Chuzzlewit*, p. 708)

Other excessive females, however, can turn even apparently well-
run households into places of discomfort and distress. The meal
prepared for Gabriel Varden and Joe Willett, Dolly's suitor, is made
inedible by one of Mrs Varden's tantrums:

> 'I'm sorry to see that you don't take your tea, Varden, and that you
> don't take yours, Mr. Joseph; though of course it would be foolish of me
> to expect that anything that can be had at home, and in the company of
> females would please *you*.' (*Barnaby Rudge*, p. 105)

The claim to represent all unregarded wives stresses the fact that it is
femaleness that spoils the food, as the narrator laboriously reiterates
in his comment on this speech:

> The pronoun was understood in the plural sense, and included both
> gentlemen, upon both of whom it was rather hard and undeserved, for
> Gabriel had applied himself to the meal with a very promising appetite,
> until it was spoilt by Mrs. Varden herself, and Joe had as great a liking
> for the female society of the locksmith's house – or for a part of it . . . as
> man could well entertain. (*Barnaby Rudge*, p. 105)

Not surprisingly, in this language the recommended cure for Mrs
Varden's power to deprive people of their proper pleasure in food is

supposed to be 'remedies in themselves nauseous and unpalatable', taking the shape of tumbling 'some half-dozen rounds in the world's ladder' (p. 54).

Mrs Joe, in *Great Expectations*, possesses this capacity to turn domestic comfort to distress to a higher degree even than Mrs Varden. For Pip even the sight of her cutting longed-for bread and butter has associations as painful as that of an apothecary preparing a plaster (p. 8). And when he and Joe have their slices served, it is done 'as if we were two thousand troops on a forced march instead of a man and boy at home' (p. 19). The very Christmas dinner, luscious in itself, reaches Pip as 'the scaly tips of the drumsticks of the fowls, . . . with those obscure corners of pork of which the pig, when living, had least reason to be vain' (p. 22). Added to the physical pain that Mrs Joe inflicts on Pip with the wax-ended cane, Tickler, is that which she manages to cause by her gift for transforming the symbols of domestic order, such as food and washing, into torment: 'Mrs. Joe was a very clean housekeeper, but had an exquisite art of making her cleanliness more uncomfortable and unacceptable than dirt itself' (*Great Expectations*, p. 20). Similarly, Mrs Wilfer in *Our Mutual Friend* perverts the celebration of her twenty-fifth wedding anniversary so that it is 'kept morally rather as a Fast than a Feast'.

The unnatural domesticity created by excessive females also figures the emotional havoc they impose on those around them. Caddy Jellyby, for instance, is made wretched and surly by the way that her mother derides her decision to marry a dancing-master instead of continuing as helper in her African project and marrying the philanthropic Mr Quale, with his 'large shining knobs for temples'. Edith Dombey, though she acquiesces in her mother's plan to sell her off to Dombey as his second wife, does so with a deep sense of her own degradation. Caddy is almost turned into another monster of unwomanliness through her mother's influence but is redeemed by Esther's affection and speedy domestic instruction.

Both this damage and the domestic disorders described above signify what happens when female nature, left to itself, tries to overthrow the proper order of things and to control where it should simply provide and influence. It represents a threat to male governance by removing the order that it should bring. As the narrator makes clear, it offers a radical threat to men and to husbands in particular. Even the resilient Gabriel Varden is diminished by his attempts to conciliate his wife's unreasonable histrionics. In the early stages of *Barnaby*

Rudge he is repeatedly intimidated by her manipulative fits of temperament and rebuked by her for his efforts at appeasement. This is nothing to the state of Joe Gargery, whose place as the head of his household has been completely usurped by Mrs Joe. His status, like Pip's, is that of a child: he too has his slices of bread and butter grudgingly doled out and is sent to church; and though not beaten by Tickler, he dreads his wife's 'Rampages'. Further, unlike Pip, he meekly accepts all this and never rebels. His destiny, as Pip sees it, is the kitchen door-step to which he is regularly banished when his wife is 'vigorously reaping the floors of her establishment' (p. 19). Eventually Pip, like Mrs Joe, despises him: the rightful order is overthrown crucially and yet more pointedly here.

The worst excesses of female tyranny are visible in the figures of Mr Jellyby and Mr Wilfer, both of whom have been reduced to that state of helplessness more appropriate to women than men. It is Mr Jellyby who maintains an unmanly (womanly) silence and who is barely identifiable at the dinner-table when Esther first visits the house. He is so badly in need of the administrative skills that his wife squanders on Africa that he is in danger of bankruptcy. A later visit is disrupted by 'Mr. Jellyby's breaking away from the dining-table, and making rushes at the window, with the intention of throwing himself into the area, whenever he made any new attempt to understand his affairs' (*Bleak House*, p. 334). His suicidal depression is compounded by the disorder he returns home to – 'bills, dirt, waste, noise, tumbles downstairs, confusion, and wretchedness' (p. 185). He weeps at the news of Caddy's engagement, believing that the best prospect for his remaining children would be 'their being all Tomahawked together' (p. 416). Even when his debts are paid he remains reduced to the status of a child and 'almost always sat when he was at home with his head against the wall' (p. 420). His inability to speak is now even more marked: 'He opened his mouth now, a great many times, and shook his head in a melancholy manner' (p. 421). Caddy recognises him as 'some poor dull child in pain' and leaves him after her wedding seeking his usual consolation, head against the wall (p. 424).

This emasculation of the male by the excessive female is re-enacted by the Wilfers with the same result: the long-suffering husband resigns the role of master to his wife and is left only with the option of regressing to childhood. Wilfer, like Gargery, wishes only to mollify his wife but cannot alter her tyrannical nature. Already so boyish in appearance as to be a temptation to schoolmasters to cane him, he soon shrinks for protection into a childishness that is fostered by his daughter, Bella. He becomes not a man but a kind of pet whom she teases; sends out to buy new clothes; and treats to the time of his life by taking him out to dinner at Greenwich in his new suit.

Thus excessive females do more than claim for themselves simple agency: if not widows, they seize power illegitimately from their husbands, reducing them to the status of non-persons, disrupting their households and damaging the other inmates in the process. But typically in Dickens' narratives disorder turns to order in the end; chaos rights itself. In the outcome, though Gargery, Jellyby and Wilfer are not returned to power, women are chastened, tamed, silenced or even destroyed. Sometimes their unnatural power is removed with a violence so in excess of their defects as to be savagely punitive; and like the threatening of nubile girls it is lingered over by the male narrators.

It is always external forces, unrelated to their conduct, that bring them to heel, as if such silencing were a natural law for the punishment of female subversion. A spurious suggestion of causation is evoked: that conduct causes this result. To an extent the reversal women undergo is graduated to match how excessive their utterance and behaviour have been. Consequently, Mrs Nickleby's takes merely the form of a series of snubs. Her silencing begins when her desire to be centre-stage in the grieving for Smike's death, 'after her own peculiar fashion of considering herself foremost' (p. 791), is thwarted by Kate's more genuine grief and the authentic hysteria of soft-hearted Miss La Creevy, a middle-aged nonentity. She is pushed further aside when, with her own ridiculous hopes of marriage dashed, she suffers the humiliation of seeing Miss La Creevy become engaged to a respectable clerk. Her mild tyranny over Kate is overthrown by her daughter's escape from Ralph Nickleby and marriage to the man of her choice. She is last seen in old age when her prattling advice is reported, not reproduced, by the narrator and ignored by those who hear it.

Like Kate Nickleby, Caddy Jellyby shakes off her mother's yoke by marrying Prince Turveydrop. She rejects the husband Mrs Jellyby has chosen for her and provides a temporary haven for the rest of the family. Esther provides the necessary gloss on this: 'I have heard that Mrs. Jellyby was understood to suffer great mortification, from her daughter's ignoble marriage and pursuits' (p. 878). Events combine further against this female orator when her African projects simultaneously fail in a ludicrous way: 'She has been disappointed in

Borrioboola-Gha, which turned out a failure in consequence of the King of Borrioboola wanting to sell everybody – who survived the climate – for Rum' (*Bleak House*, p. 878). She is reduced to the self-evidently ridiculous project of furthering 'the rights of women to sit in Parliament'.

Mrs Wilfer's defeat and silencing is also brought about by the marriage of a daughter against her wishes when Bella marries Rokesmith, and her original disapproval is rendered ridiculous by the discovery that he is immensely rich. Wronged by the very wealth and social position craved for, she ignominiously leaves the scene of Bella's triumph in a manner which makes it difficult to say 'whether it was with the air of going to the scaffold herself, or of leaving the inmates of the house for immediate execution' (*Our Mutual Friend*, p. 807). Though the triumphantly submissive marriages of Caddy and Bella do not restore male dominance to their fathers, they overthrow their mothers' attempts to determine events and they provide refuges from them that are limitations on female tyranny.

The silencing of the women discussed so far is a mild matter, but then their vocal excesses were never extreme. Mrs Varden's was verbally more exaggerated, involving as it did the fantasy and inordinate theatricality that her servant, Miggs, supports so deftly. In her case the form that corrective force takes is the abduction of her only child, Dolly, by lustful rioters. And it is the restoration of Dolly which silences her: she becomes 'an altered woman – the riots had done that good' (*Barnaby Rudge*, p. 553). The extent and nature of the alteration is revealed when the treacherous Miggs reappears and tempts her to the old histrionic indignation against her husband. For she remains uncharacteristically silent, and when Gabriel leaves Miggs' fate in her hands her answer is strikingly brief: 'I am astonished – I am amazed at her audacity. Let her leave the house this moment' (p. 616). Her rejection of Miggs represents the rejection of her own clamorous appropriation of Gabriel's mastery. Her submission to him is complete and the last reference to her is to her new silence.

A similar dramatic change takes place in Mrs Gamp when her linguistic dictatorship is overthrown by Betsey Prig's revelation that the authenticating witness, Mrs Harris, whom she so often cites, is non-existent. When Jonas Chuzzlewit subsequently entrusts her with the guardianship of Old Chuffey, who knows his murderous secret, he asks her for the name of her supposed assistant. She is now barely able to gasp out the name Harris:

It was extraordinary how much effort it cost Mrs. Gamp to pronounce the name she was commonly so ready with. She made some three or four gasps before she could get it out; and when she had uttered it, pressed her hand upon her side, and turned up her eyes as if she were going to faint away. (*Martin Chuzzlewit*, p. 775)

The pain of this silencing is symbolic of the later loss of power to harm when Old Martin Chuzzlewit acts as *deus ex machina* in revealing Pecksniff's hypocrisy and villainy and Mrs Gamp's true nature (p. 814).

But the deflation of Mrs Nickleby, Mrs Jellyby, Mrs Wilfer, Mrs Varden and Mrs Gamp is nothing to the impact of external and arbitrary forces upon Mrs Skewton and Mrs Joe Gargery. Mrs Skewton has imposed a loveless marriage to Dombey on Edith and as it falls apart she herself disintegrates physically and mentally in scenes intertwined with the marital pair's increasing hostility to each other. She is repeatedly dismantled physically by the narrator's stress on her parody of girlishness in a way that is seen at its most venomous after she suffers a mild stroke. Edith hurries to her room and finds her

arrayed in full dress, with diamonds, short sleeves, rouge, curls, teeth, and other juvenility, all complete; but Paralysis was not to be deceived . . . and had struck her at her glass, where she lay like a horrible doll that had tumbled down. (*Dombey and Son*, p. 507)

By this paralytic stroke she is deprived of the speech that was her weapon, capable only of 'inarticulate sounds'. Though she makes a partial recovery, it is now with her power gone that she falls prey to real delusions, which, unlike those of Mrs Varden and Mrs Gamp, cannot be banished but remain to torment her: her tyranny has destroyed Edith's life, yet now she longs for her daughter's love and for recognition as the perfect mother she never was.

During her half-recovery the fluent and manipulative talker of old is harassed by mental lapses that create verbal effects echoing ironically those of her earlier state when she affected vagueness. Now she really does confuse her sons-in-law Granger and Dombey as 'Grangeby' and 'Domber'; and remembers only mutilated forms of words. This cruelly protracted narrative describes the worst effects of ageing but is interpreted as an appropriate linguistic and moral punishment, caused by her former female sins, which lasts until a second stroke ends it.

Mrs Joe Gargery's silencing is no less violent and hers too is cruelly drawn out with relish by the narrator. Pip finds her 'lying without sense or movement on the bare boards where she had been knocked down by a tremendous blow on the back of the head, dealt by some unknown hand' (*Great Expectations*, p. 112). Though the hand turns out to be that of Joe's journeyman, Orlick, he is usually regarded as Pip's surrogate, inflicting the vengeance for his own and Joe's suffering that her brother desires. Certainly, her state with sight disturbed, hearing impaired and 'speech unintelligible' (p. 115) turns her into the child that Joe has long been. It is now she who is dependent and terrified. She remains incapable of proper speech until a death recorded unemotionally in the text by a letter from an undertaker to Pip. Like Mrs Skewton, she is both silenced and physically punished. Joe is freed first from the tyranny of which her speech was symbolic and then by her death for a new marriage with the biddable Biddy. So, apparently, perish all tyrants; or at least those driven to tyranny by excessive femaleness. Their subduing, silencing and destruction play what is offered as a necessary and enjoyable part in the usual restoration of order in Dickens' novels. It thus constitutes a savage attack on the very essence of femaleness which is theoretically privileged in the depiction of nubile girls.

Chapter 5

Passionate women

Their negative and positive significance

Three women, already married when the story begins (Lady Dedlock) or relatively soon after (Edith Dombey and Louisa Bounderby),
are manifestly examples of a sign with a different significance from
those discussed earlier. Their sexual status as non-virgins serves to
distinguish them from nubile girls; and their marital status as wives
from unmarried fallen girls, though Auerbach (1982) in her influential discussion collapses all fallen women into one group. This is the
reason for my choice of the term *women*. But they are equally sharply
differentiated from the range of married women described in the
last chapter whose voices proclaim their untamed femaleness. They
draw overt narratorial admiration not derision, despite (or possibly
because of) a connection with illicit sexual experience.

The form that the connection takes is, significantly, negative and
might be described as near-miss adultery. Tanner (1979) points out
that in many early nineteenth-century novels dealing with this kind of
transgression 'the actual adulterous act . . . is not described' (p. 13).
The novels that I am dealing with take this 'absence' one stage further
still to create a distinctly negative idiom in which to handle the whole
subject. Edith Dombey elopes to France with Carker, and has a scene
alone with him at an inn where he arrives to embrace 'Madame' and
to address her 'in the French tongue as his charming wife' (p. 721).
The supper for two, the adjacent bedroom, the dismissal of the
servants and all the circumstances spell out to the innkeeper and to

87

the world at large that Edith is an adulteress. Similarly, Louisa
Bounderby is seen descending 'a mighty Staircase with a dark pit of
shame and ruin at the bottom' (p. 201) until the crucial moment when
she is observed, apparently willing, in the arms of her lover, James
Harthouse:

> Mrs. Sparsit saw him detain her with his encircling arm, and heard
> him . . . tell her how he loved her, and how she was the stake for which
> he ardently desired to play away all that he had in life . . . all was alike
> to him, so that she was true to him, – the man who had seen how cast
> away she was, whom she had inspired at their first meeting with an
> admiration . . . of which he had thought himself incapable, whom she
> had received into her confidence, who was devoted to her and adored
> her. (*Hard Times*, Bk 2, p. 212)

Like the watchers at the inn in France, Mrs Sparsit, Bounderby's
housekeeper, makes the obvious interpretation: 'Lo, Louisa coming
out of the house! Hastily cloaked and muffled, and stealing away. She
elopes!' (p. 213). Over a more extended period Lady Dedlock is
watched by Guppy and Tulkinghorn for signs which will betray the
guilty 'secret' of her illegitimate daughter. Of this secret she herself
says to Esther that it is 'wretched and dishonouring', not just to
herself but to her husband. It is always treated by Tulkinghorn as a
'family secret', which, if revealed, would be as much a betrayal of Sir
Leicester as if her liaison had taken place after her marriage not
before. And this is an interpretation that she accepts.

Yet in all three novels there is an explicit negative: Edith rejects
Carker (allegedly at the prompting of Dickens' friend, Lord Jeffrey,
who refused to believe that Edith became Carker's mistress (Forster
1872–4: 2, p. 336)), Louisa runs away to her father not to Harthouse
and Lady Dedlock's affair with Hawdon is revealed to have taken
place before she met her husband. These women are *not* adulteresses;
adultery remains putative not actual. However, the prominence that
it is given, combined with the powerful taboo attaching even to the
mention of it in a woman, suggests that the negatives here are to be
treated as Freud argued those of patients should be when such
dangerous issues as this one are at stake: ' "You ask who this person in
the dream can be. It's *not* my mother." We emend this to: "So it *is* his
mother" ' (in Strachey 1961: 235). Effectively, Edith, Lady Dedlock
and Louisa are wives 'guilty' of adultery and so appropriately described as *passionate*, a term used by Slater (1983: 259ff.) but, in his

case, to refer to a broad category of what he calls 'strong-minded women'.

As indicated in chapter 3, such transgression was, traditionally, in non-fictional works explicitly reserved for the unmarried (and for the lower classes). Hemyng contrasts English wives with French (and other 'continental') married women whose chastity and faithfulness 'are remarkable by their absence' (Mayhew 1861–2: 258). The married state was discussed as a haven to be risen (or not risen) to rather than a place to be fallen from. Reference to even the existence of adulteresses was always minimal. Ellis in a half-mention subsumes them under examples of those to be castigated for acting on impulse: 'The unfaithful wife does this, when she allows her thoughts to wander from her rightful lord' (Ellis 1845: 28). This translation of physical infidelity into mental disloyalty renders even this reference ambiguous enough to be wilfully misread. Denial of the fact of female adultery was one way of containing dangerous issues like that of women's sexuality and the necessity for a double standard which would protect the legitimacy of a man's heirs. But in the period leading up to the Matrimonial Causes Act of 1857 (which made divorce possible without an Act of Parliament), the discussion of adultery did become a public focus for 'competing beliefs concerning the nature of bourgeois marriage [and] the validity of the double standard' (Nead 1988: 52).

Visual representations of the adulteress remained rare until the later 1850s but putative (or non-)adultery was the form in which the subject was addressed in at least three novels written at about the time when Dickens created his first non-adulteress, Edith Dombey. Geraldine Jewsbury's *Zoe* (1845) and Dinah Mulock Craik's *The Ogilvies* (1846) precede all three of his near-miss adultery novels; Jewsbury's *The Half Sisters* (1848) postdates *Dombey and Son* (1846–8) but predates *Bleak House* (1852–3) and *Hard Times* (1854). The fact that in all six novels adultery is projected for a woman means that sexual transgression is being considered in its strongest form, and that most subject to taboo. Even after the 1857 Act, adultery committed by a wife was alone grounds for divorce, whereas an adulterous husband had to provide other aggravating grounds for his wife to divorce him. The subject was a powerful, even an explosive, one, and if Dickens is measured against the near-adultery novels of his contemporaries, Jewsbury and Craik, it can be seen that he maximises its impact by developing the language of negation. Where they to some extent break out of the negative mode he exploits it in a way that gives it all the force of the repressed. As Freud explains in the passage already quoted:

> Negation is a way of taking cognizance of what is repressed . . . : with the help of the symbol of negation, thinking frees itself from the restrictions of repression and enriches itself with material that is indispensable for its proper functioning. (in Strachey 1961: 235)

In this case it is being suggested that it is the novelistic language for representing women which suppresses certain material that individuals like Dickens filter in by means of negative expression. In such forms it has, like irony and other forms of understatement, an ambiguous intensity.

The first instance of the linguistic difference between Dickens and the other two novelists is found in the way that the 'passion' of the (non-)adulteresses is conveyed. In *Zoe* the eponymous heroine marries the rich and elderly Gifford to escape from a restricted life with her strict English father and to acquire 'the freedom and privileges of a married woman' (1845/1989: 102). Significantly, her desire to escape is still an expression of a 'foreign' nature, since she is the illegitimate daughter of a beautiful Greek girl, from whom she also inherits exuberant intelligence and vitality. It is this foreign temperament which leads her into a tempestuous attachment to a failed Catholic priest, Everhard Burrows, towards whom she finds herself passionately attracted, physically as well as intellectually. The scene in which the ghost of their adultery is openly raised takes place after a fire in the house, during Gifford's absence, when Burrows wakes Zoe, who falls fainting into his arms. Later in the chapel,

> Zoe opened her eyes, and saw Everhard bending over her. The colour rushed over her face and neck. Everhard made an effort to turn away, but, almost unconsciously, he fell on his knees beside her; and the next moment Zoe's burning arms were round his neck, and her long hair fell like a veil over him. Everhard's brain was in a whirl, and his veins ran fire, as he felt her warm breath upon him. (1845/1989: 245).

Zoe's sexual accessibility is indicated by her loosened and encompassing hair, and their mutual desire (for which the luridly described fire in the house is now revealed as a surrogate) by the hot colour that rushes to Zoe's face, by her 'burning arms', by the way that Everhard's 'veins ran fire'. In contemporary terms their 'fiery' and guilty passion is made outrageously explicit. But the ghost of adultery is exorcised by the morally ever-hard Burrow's conscience-stricken departure; and consummation never takes place. Jewsbury, while retaining the traditional connection between illicit physical passion and non-Englishness, has asserted its existence in wives only as an aspect of a foreign and extraordinary nature. She has also done so in a way that remains at the level of the overtly sensational.

In her other novel, *The Half Sisters*, another putative adulteress appears as part of a schematic demonstration that an unconventional and passionate woman may be morally stronger than a conventional one. The half sisters of the title, Bianca, the illegitimate and half-Italian daughter of Phillip Helmsby, and her legitimate English sister, Alice, are the exponents of this scheme. It is Bianca, a gifted actress, who maintains a passionate but chaste attachment to a snobbish Englishman, Conrad Percy; while the staider Alice, ignored by her dull and wealthy husband Bryant, decides to elope with the infatuated Percy. He, perversely, is attracted by her womanly chasteness, and in Bryant's absence urges her to elope:

> Alice neither spoke nor moved, but a flash of gladness like sunlight passed over her face. Neither of them spoke. A passionate, guilty joy was in their hearts; they were interpenetrated with each other's presence.
>
> 'As the melting fire burneth,'
>
> honour, conscience, every barrier that was between them was destroyed; they only felt they were together; neither regret nor doubt intruded. THEY WERE TOGETHER. That was the one reality into which their whole life was absorbed. (Jewsbury 1848: 2, 130)

Alice's blushing and the 'fire' between the two of them code desire; adultery seems imminent but the interpenetration remains metaphorical. What might be read as a euphemism for the act itself turns into a plan for elopement. Only Bryant's sudden return prevents it, and precipitates Alice's death from a physical seizure that signals guilt and disappointment simultaneously. This novel collapses into bathos.

Though Craik's treatment of near-adultery is less bold than Jewsbury's, she still uses positive, not negative, language in treating illicit female desire. Her putative adulteress, Katherine Ogilvie, is not given the excuse of foreign birth but like Alice Bryant is entirely English. However, her passion for the meretricious Paul Lynedon, which revives after her loveless marriage, is, like Zoe's, the outcome of a vivacious and emotional temperament. There is, even in Craik's coded handling, no doubt of her physical response when, in her husband's absence, Lynedon declares his love, and the tell-tale sign of 'burning crimson' rushes to her brow. Although she is quick to dismiss him, the violent pain she feels after he has gone tropes her passion directly:

> [she] sank back exhausted and lay for a long time almost senseless. Again and again there darted through her side that sharp arrowy pain – which she had first felt after the night when a few chance words . . . had swept away all hope and love for ever from her life. Of late this pain had been more frequent and intense. (Craik 1848: 369)

The pangs of desire are displaced onto what turns out to be a fatal heart disease which returns the narrative to the idea of death as punishment for sexual transgression.

Coded though it is, the language of these three novels describes, in a positive form, the presence of an illicit physical passion in the three wives involved, even though conventional plots work to cancel its significance. What Dickens does in the treatment of his (non-)adulteresses is to strengthen the negative language in which their passion is represented and so paradoxically to increase its importance. He then involves them in plots which shift their significance further. Though his three women are, like the three just discussed, revealed as creatures of passionate feelings, these are not explicitly sexual, or rather they are explicitly not-sexual; and as Freud said, statements on such subjects can be emended to be read as strongly positive. Thus Edith's strongest passion is directed towards her stepdaughter, Florence, and it is through playing on this surrogate love that Carker manipulates her into near-adultery. Her fiercely passionate nature is demonstrated when, after her pseudo-elopement with Carker, she threatens him with a knife:

> 'I have something lying here, that is no love trinket; and sooner than endure your touch once more, I would use it on you – and you know it, while I speak – with less reluctance than I would on any other creeping thing that lives. . . . How many times in your smooth manner, and mocking words and looks, have I been twitted with my courtship and my marriage?' (*Dombey and Son*, p. 723)

In powerfully suggestive tropes she speaks of him 'laying bare' her 'wound of love' and 'lacerating' it; and concludes histrionically: 'How often have you fanned the fire on which, for two years, I have writhed?' Pain and fire, obvious, even trite, terms of sexual desire in Jewsbury and Craik, are redeployed ambiguously to signal ostensibly resentment and thwarted maternal love, feelings which can respectably be articulated. They make of Edith a woman as 'passionate' as Zoe, Alice or Katherine.

Similarly, Lady Dedlock's hidden feelings are diverted into a desperate love for her illegitimate daughter, Esther Summerson, where, like Edith's feelings for Florence, they can legitimately be expressed, a technique displayed more fully in novels to be treated in chapter 6. In Esther's reporting, their force is revealed in a string of negatives better suited to the separation of lovers:

> We never could associate, never could communicate, never probably from that time forth could interchange another word, on earth. . . . If I could believe that she loved me, in this agony in which I saw her, with a mother's love, she asked me to do that; for then I might think of her with a greater pity, imagining what she suffered. She had put herself beyond all hope, and beyond all help . . . no affection could come near her, and no human creature could render her any aid. (*Bleak House*, pp. 510–11)

Lady Dedlock's residual affection/anguish for her former lover Nemo-Hawdon is a discreet reflection of this pain/desire.

When Louisa Bounderby almost succumbs to James Harthouse's seduction, it is pain that figures her desire in her final 'confession' to her father:

> 'But if you ask me whether I have loved him, or do love him, I tell you plainly, father, that it may be so. I don't know.'
> She took her hands suddenly from his shoulders, and pressed them both upon her side; while in her face, not like itself – and in her figure, drawn up, resolute to finish by a last effort what she had to say – the feelings long suppressed broke loose. (*Hard Times*, Bk 2, pp. 218–19)

In the telling of these feelings she equates them not only with possible love for Harthouse but with all those aspects of her emotional nature that Gradgrind has taught her from childhood to repress, all 'the sensibilities, affections, weaknesses', 'the hunger and thirst' for imaginative experience, the 'ardent impulse towards some region where rules, and figures and definitions were not quite absolute' (Bk 2, pp. 216ff.).

However, despite Dickens' displacement of passion into non-sexual areas, its sexual nature is signalled powerfully and covertly through the medium of guilt. The most prominent example of this is the sense of deep shame (and resentment) that the three women share with the fallen girls described in chapter 3. Like her *alter ego*, Alice Marwood, Edith displays to her mother horror and indignation at what she has become when she sells herself to Dombey. She feels unfairly deprived of her chance of womanliness, her opportunity to develop 'the germ of all that purifies a woman's breast' (p. 382):

> 'When was I a child! What childhood did you ever leave to me? I was a woman – artful, designing, mercenary, laying snares for men – before I knew myself, or you, or even understood the base and wretched aim of every new display I learnt.' (*Dombey and Son*, p. 381)

Louisa Bounderby, in 'confessing' to her father, also speaks of herself as a former nubile girl, in the language used for their description. The fallen woman's conventional resentment and shame appear as wild regret for 'the spring and summer' of her girlhood, robbed from her by the 'frost and blight that have hardened and spoiled' her. These forces have, strikingly, 'crushed my better angel into a demon' (*Hard Times*, Bk 2, pp. 216–17). Like the fallen girls, and like Edith and Lady Dedlock, she naturally shrinks from female innocence, represented for her by Sissy Jupe, the still angelic circus girl. The biblical language of condemnation reappears in the allusion to bad seed in the narratorial comment on her 'wicked' reaction to Sissy's pity after her own putative fall:

> A dull anger that she should be seen in her distress . . . smouldered within her like an unwholesome fire. . . . So in her bosom even now; the strongest qualities she possessed, long turned upon themselves, became a heap of obduracy, that rose against a friend. (*Hard Times*, Bk 3, p. 224)

Added to the harlot's shame is the usual small but significant detail signalling sexual accessibility: scenes in which Edith, Lady Dedlock and Louisa appear in an intimate state with hair hanging loose. With Edith this happens in her final confrontation with Dombey before the supposed elopement when she tears off her jewelled tiara, 'plucking it off with a force that dragged and strained her rich black hair with heedless cruelty', and brings it 'tumbling wildly on her shoulders' (p. 631) in a way pointedly reminiscent of Alice Marwood's. Lady Dedlock's public air of propriety is never shattered until she is found dead at the graveyard with the 'long dank hair' of a fallen woman. But after Tulkinghorn has confronted her with his intention of revealing her guilty secret she privately and frenziedly paces her own room with 'her hair wildly thrown from her flung-back face' (p. 581). More oblique is Louisa's scene in her brother Tom's bedroom when she urges him to confess his robbery and lies with her hair 'flowing over him as if she would hide him'. Her intense love for Tom expands to include Harthouse, who, by feigning an interest in her brother, is able to work on her affection, rather as Carker works on Edith's feelings for Florence. His conscious intention of taking her brother's place in her affections reflects strangely on the sibling relationship. Then, conclusively, after the confession to her father of her (non-)adulterous affair with Harthouse she is seen on her bed 'with scattered hair'.

This covert connection with illicit desire, combined with the overt signs of a magdalen, has two results: the first is the suggestion of a wickedness beyond naming; the second, the striking implication that the three women possess a powerful secret, fascinatingly inaccessible to the many observers. This paradoxical effect is enacted also in the way that their appearance, always crucial in the language of representation, is described. Like nubile girls, the three women are flawlessly beautiful; and like most other women in Dickens' novels, their beauty is of an unspecific kind. Edith is 'very handsome', 'so beautiful', 'beautiful and stately', 'proud and dignified'. At a glance she is infinitely 'writable' and the observer may fill in the details to taste. But on a closer look the limits of interpretation are shown to be narrow. With each general reference to Edith's beauty comes a gloss that reads it as adamantine: she is 'beautiful and stately' but 'so cold'; her 'pride and dignity' express 'scorn and bitterness'; her beauty is twice described as 'repellent'. And similarly disjunctive language recurs in the descriptions of Lady Dedlock and Louisa. First come the generalised adjectives: Lady Dedlock is 'pretty rather than handsome', 'as graceful as she was beautiful', her eyes are 'handsome', as is her face. But almost invariably these descriptions are read off as manifestations of hauteur, pride and defiance. Her 'imperious chilling air' denies the accessibility that the adjectives suggest. Louisa's appearance, less frequently referred to in a more sparing text, presents the same verbal offer of a 'writable' charm that is quickly withdrawn. She is 'graceful and pretty' but 'impassive, cold and proud'; her features are handsome but always 'their natural play was so locked up, that it seemed impossible to guess at their genuine expression' (Bk 2, p. 127). Unlike the nubile girls with whom they share this quality of feminine beauty, they are neither writable nor iterable. They are self-contained, unique and tantalisingly unreadable: they resist the very appropriation which they invite.

This distinctiveness is enhanced by their positive failure to relate in any of the predictable (positive or negative) ways to their domestic setting: they are not basic providers like Mrs Toodle or Mrs Bagnet, not disruptive forces like excessive females, not delightful edibles like nubile girls. They neither sustain domesticity nor wreck it, but simply remain aloof from it. From the opening of *Bleak House* Lady Dedlock is a centrepiece and household god, the most ornamental of the Dedlock possessions; while Edith and Louisa take on the same passive roles when they marry and move into their rich husband's houses. Their necessary connection, as women, with food is tenuous, and those around them are seldom allowed to eat. 'Soup and fish' are mentioned at Bounderby's dinner for Harthouse, largely as a means of illustrating the host's innate vulgarity when they cause him to reminisce about the 'polonies and saveloys' (Bk 2, p. 130) of his youth. But Louisa is never seen to order or to eat food. In *Bleak House* the goods with which tradesmen tempt Lady Dedlock do not include anything edible; 'wine-drinking', but apparently not eating, takes place in Paris; Boodle, Coodle and Doodle, when entertained by the Dedlocks, appear to dine off each other; the household and its guests live on 'leaden lunches' and 'dismal dinners'. When Lady Dedlock 'dines' alone in her room, of course, she 'eats nothing'.

In *Dombey and Son* the dinner table is a central feature but rather as a battlefield for Edith and Dombey than as a source of nourishment. It is remarkable for its glitter, its gold and silver cutlery, with food to match. It is pictured as 'a long plateau of precious metal frosted' (p. 491), and those who dine off it enjoy a strange menu: 'rich meats and wines', followed by 'continual gold and silver, dainties of earth, air, fire and water, and that unnecessary article in Mr. Dombey's banquets – ice' (p. 493). Their refusal to act in a womanly way as providers or even in an unwomanly way as spoilers of food leaves the three (non-)adulteresses as female anomalies. They neither dispense nor act as roast goose, nor do they spoil joints of beef but instead preside over meals where opulence replaces food: objects are substituted for nourishment. Though not equatable in the normal way with food, these women are equated with the consumer goods that surround them.

This is true in a literal and bad sense, as the narrator makes clear;

their household furnishings, clothes, jewels and other possessions are the price paid for them by husbands whom they do not love. The purchase of Lady Dedlock is evinced by the conspicuous furnishings, paintings and statuary at Chesney Wold and at the town house, 'a world wrapped up in too much jeweller's cotton and fine wool' (*Bleak House*, p. 8). Bounderby's wooing of Louisa Gradgrind takes the form of handing over equivalent goods:

> Love was made on these occasions in the form of bracelets, and on all occasions during the period of betrothal, took a manufacturing aspect. Dresses were made, jewellery was made, cakes and gloves were made, settlements were made, an extensive assortment of Facts did appropriate honour to the contract. (*Hard Times*, Bk 1, p. 107)

As well as underlining the contract which these adulteresses are so dramatically (not) to transgress, these objects have an ambiguous force. As the price for sexual favours they are ostensibly disapproved of by the narrator, but the mysterious decadence that their richness, gaudiness or opulence indicates holds a powerful attraction for him.

This is particularly true of Edith's objects, which are finer than Louisa's and more directly hers than Lady Dedlock's: her rich belongings speak of a glamorous corruption that belongs to both. When Carker and Dombey dismantle her with their gaze into the luxurious and exotic things that she uses or wears, they itemise her linguistically as men usually itemise nubile girls. Dombey sees her in 'chaplets of flowers, plumes of feathers, jewels, laces, silks and satins . . . riches, despised, and poured out' (p. 541); Carker sees 'the feathers of a beautiful bird's wing showering upon the floor' as she plucks them from 'a pinion of some rare and beautiful bird, which hung from her wrist by a golden thread'. Edith as phoenix lends herself readily to the narrator's perception of her as a being whose diamonds are part of her body and as likely as she to turn pale during a dangerous interview with Dombey (pp. 600ff.). But significantly, she controls the diamonds, not the other way round. 'The wealth of colour and voluptuous glitter' of her surroundings is 'repeated' and outshone by her 'repellent' beauty. The blend of the corrupt and the magnificent is seen as having a peculiar magnetism.

This power to attract through a combination of moral taint, resistance and glitter is enhanced by the way that each woman reclaims a specific identity for herself through her evident choice of a single object, from those that surround her, as the expression of a concealed self. With Edith this is the looking glass: from her first appearance walking by her mother's wheeled chair she presents herself to the world as a figure of invincible haughtiness for whom there is nothing in all the world 'worth looking into, save a mirror' (p. 280). Her refusal to offer anything more of herself than an ambiguous image is consolidated by the only picture given back by the 'broad high mirrors' of Dombey's house of 'a woman with a noble quality yet dwelling in her nature, who was too false to her better self . . . to save herself' (p. 409). It is only Edith through the looking-glass that Dombey is allowed to see during a critical interview in her room as 'glancing at the mirror . . . he saw immediately, as in a picture frame, the knitted brow and darkened beauty he knew so well' (p. 540). When he is eventually driven out by her scorn he looks back 'upon the well-lighted and luxurious room, the beautiful and glittering objects everywhere displayed, the shape of Edith in *its* rich dress seated before her glass, and the face of Edith as the glass presented *it* to him' (p. 546; my emphases). In this way Edith ironically depersonalises herself as his gaze so often depersonalised her. Dombey's inability to gain more purchase upon her than he can upon a reflection in a glass makes her magnetic for him. The capacity to resist hinted at in the generalised descriptions of her is heightened to a point where it becomes itself irresistibly attractive.

The same is true for Carker, when, at the French inn, he believes himself about to take physical possession of her. Edith again sits before mirrors in the lighted room which frames her like a picture:

> The glitter of bright tapers, and their reflection in looking-glasses, were confined . . . to one room. . . . Seen from the hall, where a lamp was feebly burning, through the dark perspective of open doors, it looked as shining and precious as a gem. In the heart of its radiance sat a beautiful woman – Edith. (*Dombey and Son*, p. 720)

When he penetrates the frame into this 'sanctuary of light and colour' Carker finds, like Dombey, that his possession is as delusory as the possession of a reflection in a mirror.

Lady Dedlock's self-image is that of a portrait: beautiful, immobile and commanding. Not only is she 'pictured' by others, in various ways, before her first appearance but her portrait hanging over the 'great chimney piece' dominates the long drawing room at Chesney Wold. When Guppy first sees this it works upon him 'like a charm', and, not distinguishing it from the real woman, he wanders dazed

L.O. aesthetically has the look of a proper feminine but she embodies that which would make her fallen through the house 'as if he were looking everywhere for Lady Dedlock again' (p. 88). This is an identification that she herself encourages in her public confrontations with Tulkinghorn at Chesney Wold, where she poses unmoving and unmovable, fire-screen in hand, like her own portrait. It is as though a painting had come to visit him when he sees her face framed by the glass of his door and even he is disconcerted. Once she has entered his room, with his determined composure matching hers, they 'look at each other, like two pictures' (p. 575). It has become her will to remain as unchanging as a painting, neither expressing weakness nor exciting compassion. In her interviews with Guppy she poses coldly and steadily, allowing the 'splendour and beauty of her appearance' to work its deterrent effect on his blackmailing designs. His revelation that he knows the secret of her illegitimate daughter at first merely freezes her into greater immobility:

> Lady Dedlock sits before him, looking him through, with the same dark shade upon her face, in the same attitude even to the holding of the screen, with her lips a little apart, her brow a little contracted, but, for the moment, dead. (*Bleak House*, p. 407)

Like the eyes of a portrait, her eyes hold and dominate him: 'her eyes never once release him' (p. 409).

Like the other two women, Louisa also chooses a distinctive image that is to represent her to others. It is the narrator who first describes her face showing 'a light with nothing to rest upon, a fire with nothing to burn' (Bk 1, p. 12). But she takes this image to herself at every turn in the story when she chooses to sit staring into the fire. When questioning Tom she speaks 'slowly, and in a curious tone, as if she were reading what she asked in the fire, and it were not quite plainly written there' (Bk 1, p. 53). Rebuked by her mother for 'wondering' and being asked what encouraged it, she claims to have been encouraged by nothing 'but by looking at the red sparks dropping out of the fire, and whitening and dying' (Bk 1, p. 54). After Tom has urged her to marry Bounderby and she gazes at the lurid fires of Coketown, the narrator comments that 'It seemed as if, first in her own fire within the house, and then in the fiery haze without, she tried to discover what kind of woof Old Time . . . would weave from the threads he had already spun into a woman' (*Hard Times*, Bk 1, pp. 94–5). The familiar trope for desire takes on a new force in this novel as the fire itself is expressive of mystery and of some evil. This is made clear when

Coketown again attracts and holds Louisa's gaze while Gradgrind presses Bounderby's proposal on her and asks ironically whether she is consulting the factory chimneys. She answers enigmatically that 'There seems to be nothing there but languid and monotonous smoke. Yet when the night comes, Fire bursts out, father!' (Bk 1, p. 100). Her warning goes unheeded, night comes and fire does break out in a relationship with Harthouse that destroys her marriage and much else.

After her flight from Harthouse 'dull anger' smoulders within her 'like an unwholesome fire' (Bk 3, p. 224). What the now familiar 'fires' mean is unknown even to her, and in the end Bounderby's possession of her as a wife is as delusory as Harthouse's. The three women offer themselves to the world in a form as ungraspable as a reflection in a mirror, an image in a portrait, an unquenchable fire. It is in this way that Edith, Lady Dedlock and Louisa each holds within herself a secret that constitutes an identity not granted to other women in Dickens' novels. Uniquely, they are not amenable to explanation and so to erasure as are nubile girls, fallen girls and excessive females.

The power that guards the secret and inner self of these passionate women is the one traditionally associated with female merit: the ability to keep silence. It is not that they never speak, for all three do so at moments of crisis. Edith reveals her hatred of both Carker and Dombey in histrionic speeches after the pseudo-elopement; Lady Dedlock privately struggles against the tyranny of Tulkinghorn's attempt at controlling her through his self-gratifying deferral of the revelation of her illicit affair; and Louisa finally confronts her father with an accusatory account of how he has destroyed her. On these occasions they occupy the high moral ground that is matched by that stylising of standard speech (with its rhetorical patterning and syntactic control) always underwritten by the narrator as appropriate in such circumstances. But they have the power of choosing their moments to speak and their moments not to speak, a power characteristically lacking in untutored, excessive females. And each has her own style of not speaking, making use of it to resist invasion, to protect her secret or to disturb her interlocutor. This talent is not shared by the non-adulteresses in Jewsbury's or Craik's novels.

For Edith, taciturnity becomes a powerful weapon in her struggle against Dombey, taking the form of a conscious refusal to play the prescribed role of social enabler and producer of small talk. She will not admire Dombey's ornate refurbishing of his house, nor play the role of hostess in it. At the celebratory dinner he gives for his friends she turns against him that cold indifference which had formerly captivated him. 'Those visitors whom he wished to distinguish with particular attention' she receives with 'proud coldness' and shows 'no interest or wish to please, and never, after the bare ceremony of reception, in consultation of his wishes, or in welcome of his friends, opened her lips' (p. 494). And once they are alone together she inhibits him from expressing his burning indignation by merely refusing to speak:

> If his handsome wife had reproached him . . . or broken the silence in which she remained, by one word . . . Mr. Dombey would have been equal to some assertion of his case against her. But the intense, unutterable, withering scorn, with which . . . she dropped her eyes as if he were too worthless and indifferent to her to be challenged with a syllable . . . he had no resource against. (*Dombey and Son*, p. 500)

She again resorts to silence when he visits her in her bedroom and demands from her 'an improved sense of duty'. She answers 'not one word' and he sees

> no more expression of any heed of him, in the mirror, than if he had been an unseen spider on the wall, or beetle on the floor, or rather, than if he had been the one or other, seen and crushed when she last turned from him, and forgotten among the ignominious and dead vermin of the ground. (p. 546)

Their battle becomes a war to impose his words and will on her, his punishment of her is the infliction of communication through the medium of the loathsome Carker.

Lady Dedlock's silence about her past underpins the unwillingness to speak that characterises her haughty demeanour. To those who solicit answers from her she replies briefly or not at all, a fact conveyed by the narrator's practice of reporting rather than repeating what she says. Under pressure from Guppy she remains silent for as long as possible or wherever possible, thereby reducing his capacity to triumph over her. Even when it has become clear that he knows Hawdon was her lover and that Esther is her illegitimate daughter, she remains impassive and silent during most of their interview until he feels 'not only . . . conscious that he has no guide, in the least perception of what is really the complexion of her thoughts; but also that he is being every moment . . . removed further and further from her'. Her silence at this point manipulates him: 'She will not speak, it is plain. So he must' (p. 470).

Tulkinghorn understands her strategy. At first he meets her silence with speeches hinting at his knowledge of her secret, even telling the story of her liaison with Hawdon under cover of an anecdote about the mistress of another girl like her maid, Rosa. Lady Dedlock sits throughout this narrative 'perfectly still' and without a word in the moonlight that falls on her. Nor does she speak when it is over. Eventually, Tulkinghorn learns to meet silence with silence, torment-ing her by *not* revealing his knowledge of her past to her husband while leaving her under the constant threat of doing so:

> He studies her at his leisure, not speaking for a time. She too studies something at her leisure. She is not the first to speak; appearing indeed so unlikely to be so, though he stood there until midnight, that even he is driven upon breaking silence. (*Bleak House*, pp. 660–1)

To Sir Leicester she never truly speaks, leaving her expression of guilt and penitence in a farewell note: 'If I am sought for, or accused of, his murder, believe that I am wholly innocent. Believe no other good of me, for I am innocent of nothing else that you have heard, or will hear, laid to my charge' (p. 759). Her remorse, here expressed in a form that removes the directness of speech, is further distanced by reference to herself in the third person:

> 'May you . . . be able to forget the unworthy woman on whom you have wasted a most generous devotion – who avoids you, only with a deeper shame than that with which she hurries from herself and who writes this last adieu!' (*Bleak House*, p. 759)

This removal from herself is the last step to a silence that culminates in the silence of death.

Whereas Edith and Lady Dedlock impose silence upon them-selves, with Louisa it is imposed from outside by her father's injunction not to wonder and not to use her imagination but to concentrate on the facts that she finds so alien. As her mother and Tom join in the repression, however, she gradually seizes on silence as a form of self-defence, a protection for the fire within her. When her brother asks her to help him by encouraging Bounderby's suit, she resists by not replying. When urged by her father to agree, she asks a few ironic questions of which he fails to see the point, and then makes an acceptance that is striking for what it does not say: 'Let it be so. Since Mr. Bounderby likes to take me thus, I am satisfied to accept his proposal. Tell him, father . . . that this was my answer' (*Hard Times*,

Bk 2, pp. 100–1). Throughout the betrothal, the wedding prepara-
tions and the ceremony itself she is invisible and silent. Harthouse's
subsequent observation of her is necessarily purely visual as he
studies the face and manner expressive of her withdrawal, with 'her
figure in company with them there, and her mind apparently quite
alone' (Bk 2, p. 127). It is only through observing how her facial
expression changes that he realises how Tom can move her. When he
begins his seduction by feigning interest in Tom he almost moves her
to speech: 'she made a slight movement, as if she were trying to speak'
and 'seemed to try to answer but nothing came of it' (Bk 2, pp.
170–1). To some extent he induces her to break her silence and all it
implies, but he is deceived as to what she means. He interprets as
acquiescence her failure to tell him that she does not mean to elope
with him. Reticence has become her nature.

In each of the narratives it is the power not to speak and the
deliberate refusal to communicate that encodes the essential self of the
three women concerned. Not speaking is at once a means of resistance
and a form of self-definition, an ironic reversal of the stereotypical
garrulousness that renders excessive females uniformly undesirable,
knowable and despicable. Conversely, the force of reticence, the
withholding of a secret core, makes these women, for the narrator, not
iterable but unknowable and desirable.

For there is more to silence in a woman than social skill or feminine
submission; it suggests the moral and emotional fastidiousness of a
Cordelia or an Amy Dorrit. This sense of refinement is underpinned
for Dickens' (non-)adulteresses by their rank: Edith and Louisa are
certainly upper-middle class and Lady Dedlock undeniably aristo-
cratic. Such social status is generally assumed to breed the 'natural
delicacy' that Ellis refers to in speaking of how undesirable it is for
lower-middle-class women to forget their proper place when joining
in charitable work with their betters. The latter would be rightly
repelled, she thinks, by 'the least symptom of the difference of rank
being forgotten by the inferior party' (Ellis, 1843a: 218) and the
inferior party would do well to cultivate some delicacy. Any possible
low associations attached to a fallen woman finally are deleted for
Edith, Lady Dedlock and Louisa by their rank. In this way Dickens
boldly contradicts the familiar equation of sexual transgression with
low social status, justifying at least that part of Auerbach's claims
(1982) about the Victorian mythology of women in which she states
that some of them become 'the abased figurehead of a fallen culture'

(p. 157). However, she does not distinguish fallen girls from passionate women or erring wives and is mainly concerned, anyway, with pictorial grandeur.

Thus, in the significance that he attaches to these passionate women, Dickens has deployed all the available resources of the language of representation to produce a combination of meaning in which positive claims and health warnings are inextricably and fascinatingly mingled. By the narratives in which he involves them he alters their meaning in ways not envisaged by Auerbach, as will be seen in the next section. In doing so, he reveals some of the contradictions that underlie the conventional representation of them.

Narrative syntax: a mystery is (not) solved

As fallen girls are destined by traditional narrative patterns to fall even lower, the (non-)adulteresses Edith and Louisa are destined to be involved in sequences culminating in their almost, but not quite, committing adultery. Lady Dedlock's story, though more complicated, is a variant of this pattern: the revelation that she is not adulterous is accompanied by the revelation that she has committed the less heinous sin of fornication. She has half-committed adultery. But more of the story is already prescribed for Edith and Louisa than a negative peripety. Given their class and refinement, a causal explanation other than spontaneous passion has to be provided for their approach to sexual transgression. With fallen girls the usual reason given by narratives is a wicked seducer; in the novels in question here a prominent causal role is allotted to the husband.

This develops further the practice of the non-Dickensian texts which assign a mild degree of culpability to the three husbands by the use of a linguistic pattern of half-negatives. Typical is the picture of Gifford as seen by the seventeen-year-old Zoe: 'a gentlemanly-looking Englishman, of about fifty, much marked with the smallpox, but in spite of that his face had . . . a pleasing and intelligent expression' (Jewsbury 1845/1989: 96). When, under pressure from her father, Zoe agrees to marry him, the ugliness and intelligence are again counterpointed in her laconic comment that he is 'good-natured . . . and . . . not so very ugly either' (p. 100). He is rich but she does not love him; so he is suitable (and not suitable). Just so, later he is to prove a bad husband (and not a bad husband): considerate at unexpected moments (and tyrannical in destroying her French book at others), high mindedly (and culpably) trusting. He is conscientiously occupied in running his estate and in introducing 'a Catholic mission' into Devonshire (and consequently irresponsible in neglecting Zoe and introducing the fascinating priest, Burrows, into his house). Thus he is responsible (and not responsible) for Zoe's passion for Burrows.

Bryant, Alice's husband in *The Half Sisters*, is a Gifford clone: rich, middle-aged, 'solidly built' and quiet. The reassuring effect of this facade is undermined by the ironic narratorial comment on the 'charm and mystery' of such quiet people – 'all within them has the prestige of an oracle':

> Every body has felt the charm of a kind, or even of a reasonably civil expression; from one of these reserved, silent persons; 'it is not much' . . . but from so-and-so it means 'a great deal'; it is like signing a blank cheque on our self-complacency. (Jewsbury 1848: 1, 76)

He too is a good husband (and not a good husband): faithful, solid and hardworking (and abstracted, imperceptive and inflexible). When his wife is left solitary and depressed by the death of her mother he does not 'remark' it and attributes her mood to her 'fancifulness' (1, 164), so leaving her prey to the vicious but sympathetic Conrad Percy.

Similarly, though Hugh Ogilvie is of Katherine's own age and, as heir to the family estate, a good match, he is not a match for her. He is pictured as an ambiguous combination of faithful, honest lover and lout, young god and crude bucolic:

> a fine specimen of mere physical beauty – the *beau ideal* of a young country squire: most girls would have thought him a very Apollo. . . . And though somewhat rough, he was not coarse, else how could Katherine have liked him? . . . And since his affection for her had grown into the happiness of assured love, his manner had gained a softness that was almost refinement. (Craik 1846: 234–5)

Like Bryant, he neglects his wife for 'days and weeks altogether' (though possibly only because he knows he can never really win her love).

These equivocations about whose fault the near-transgression is give way in Dickens to a direct and emphatic statement of the role of at least two of the husbands in their wives' flight towards adultery.

Dombey quite openly buys Edith, as she herself stresses; and Bounderby coerces the youthful Louisa into marriage through the instrumentality of her father and brother. Even the all-too-worldly Lady
Dedlock is given a retrospective excuse for her earlier misconduct by
the manifest unsuitability of Sir Leicester, a man twenty years older
than her and, initially, a monster of pompous pride with his opinion
'that the world might get on without hills but would be done up
without Dedlocks'. This removal of much of the women's culpability
is at odds with the strong sense of taint signalled as attaching to them,
that was described in the first section of this chapter. It sharpens the
contradiction between that sense of decadence and the admiration
that they recurrently elicit from the narrator.

At the same time this equation is further affected by the rehandling
of a plot which appears, at first, to be structured as a decline which is,
like that of the fallen girl, supposed to have an irresistible momentum.
This is powerfully evoked through the speculations of the onlookers.
The idea of a vortex is captured in *Dombey and Son* in the stages marked
by Florence's perceptions of Edith:

> Little by little, she receded from Florence, like the retiring ghost of
> what she had been; little by little, the chasm between them widened
> and grew deeper; little by little, all the power of earnestness and
> tenderness she had shown, was frozen up in the bold, angry hardihood
> with which she stood, upon the brink of a deep precipice unseen by
> Florence, daring to look down. (pp. 623–4)

Similarly Mrs Sparsit's imaginings figure an irresistible fall for
Louisa:

> The figure descended the great stairs, . . . always verging, like a weight
> in deep water, to the black gulf at the bottom . . . Mrs. Sparsit saw her
> staircase, with the figure coming down. Very near the bottom now.
> Upon the brink of the abyss. . . . She falls from the lowermost stair, and
> is swallowed up in the gulf. (*Hard Times*, Bk 2, pp. 206ff.)

Lady Dedlock is seen being driven towards some catastrophe by
Tulkinghorn and then after his murder and her flight, 'overturned
and whirled away, like a leaf before a mighty wind' (p. 759). The
traditional progress of a fallen woman's decline is imagined for her by
Bucket: 'a dark, dark shapeless object drifting with the tide, more
solitary than all' (p. 767). With none of the three women does the
imagined fall ever actually take place in these terms; it remains a non-
factual (and therefore) subjunctive plot alongside the active and

indicative string of events. But it sharpens the paradoxical significance of this sign: passionate women are *not* guilty because of their
husband's offences but they *are* guilty because of their near fall into
nameless evil.

A further difference is noticeable between Dickens' plots and those
of Jewsbury and Craik. With the two women's novels the significance
of the putative fall lies in its closeness to reality, from which it is at one
moment separated by only a hair's breadth. It is used to assert that
female passion exists. The gap in Dickens is theoretically much wider:
Edith, in the published text at least, claims never to have intended
adultery, and Louisa's feelings at the crucial moment are misread by
Mrs Sparsit. Retrospectively, she too claims never to have intended
elopement. With Dickens the emphasis falls on the mystery which
remains at the heart of moral darkness that is apparently unravelled.
This is prepared for by the construction of the narrative around
attempts to unravel the enigma that Edith, Louisa and Lady Dedlock
seem to present to onlookers. These attempts provide the dynamic of
the plot, though they usually fail.

Carker does appear, at first, to decipher Edith:

> every degradation she had suffered in her own eyes was as plain to him
> as to herself . . . he read her life as though it were a vile book, and
> fluttered the leaves before her in slight looks and tones of voice which
> no one else could detect. (*Dombey and Son*, p. 502)

But when they meet in France for what he imagines will be a
'delicious' future together, he finds that he has misread her. She
has manipulated him into what looks like an elopement to revenge
herself on Dombey and to frustrate him simultaneously. She remains
'resolute', 'dauntless', 'indomitable', 'resistless': he can neither possess her nor fathom her.

The 'secret' attaching to Lady Dedlock is pursued by Guppy as
well as by Tulkinghorn, and he attempts to uncover it in many ways,
ferreting out her letters and scrutinising her for signs that he may be
able to decode. Tulkinghorn even wrangles with her about whether
the secret is hers, jealously claiming it as the Dedlocks'. After Tulkinghorn's death Bucket pursues the same quest and it is he who finds
such a solution as is found.

Louisa, though pursued by fewer detectives, is more evasive still:
her very questions reveal 'an interest gone astray like a banished
creature and hiding in solitary places' (Bk 1, p. 58). Bounderby takes

her acceptance of him at face value and is content to read her and write her off as a faithless wife. He says, when interrupting her father's assertion that he has not understood her, that he prefers his own interpretation: 'I know what I took her for, as well as you do. Never mind what I took her for; that's my look out' (*Hard Times*, Bk 3, p. 244). Her father himself assumes that he can read her mystery, or rather that there is no mystery. But she proves to be beyond his interpretation because she represents, unknown to him, 'all those subtle essences of humanity which will elude the utmost cunning of algebra' (Bk 1, p. 99). He takes her cynical acceptance of his advice that she should marry Bounderby as a sound decision, rationally arrived at, and is astounded by her 'confession'.

Even that avid reader of women, James Harthouse, finds himself baffled by Louisa's 'curious reserve'. It is her ambiguous appearance that attracts him keenly to the task of decoding her: she is 'so constrained, and yet so careless; so reserved, and yet so watchful; so cold and proud, and yet so sensitively ashamed'. Confident of success, he is content to defer the pleasure of gratification: 'It was of no use "going in" yet awhile to comprehend this girl for she baffled all penetration' (Bk 2, p. 127). He soon begins 'to read . . . with a student's eye' the resentment that he sees, unaware of 'the better and profounder part of her character' (Bk 2, p. 167). The difficulty of the text titillates his jaded senses. But his reading remains inadequate and he never penetrates her. Like Carker with Edith he fatally misreads her final intentions as acquiescence in an adulterous elopement.

After all these false dawns some kind of resolution seems finally to be arrived at when Edith leaves Dombey, when Louisa returns to her father, when Lady Dedlock, known now publicly as the mother of an illegitimate daughter but not a murderess, flees from the Dedlock home. There is at this point a sense in which a mystery has been solved: what Edith was up to with Carker, what Louisa feels about Bounderby, what Lady Dedlock's past was (though this has long been known to the reader) and who murdered Tulkinghorn. But it is *a* mystery that has been seen to be solved, not *the* mystery. Such explanation as there is remains at a superficial level of fact and event and is not a decoding of whatever the three women hold within themselves. It merely means that their secret is no longer pursued; Lady Dedlock evades her pursuers by dying, while Edith and Louisa become remote figures, guarded by neutered male relatives, Cousin Feenix and Mr Gradgrind.

More important than the spurious solving of a mystery is the cataclysm that accompanies it. After Dombey has been publicly shamed by Edith's apparent elopement, the House itself falls into decline:

> Through a whole year, the famous House of Dombey and Son had fought a fight for life, against cross accidents, doubtful rumours, unsuccessful ventures, unpropitious times, and most of all, against the infatuation of its head, who would not contract its enterprises by a hair's breath, and would not listen to a word of warning that the ship he strained so hard against the storm, was weak and could not bear it. The year was out, and the great House was down . . . Dombey and Son had stopped, and next night a List of Bankrupts [was] published, headed by that name. (p. 773)

In the same way Louisa's open defection from Bounderby is followed by (and therefore appears to cause) a public exposure of his self-aggrandising lies about his origins. Soon after that comes the prediction that his future plans will be frustrated by an ignominious death from 'a fit' in the street, leading to a contested will causing 'quibble, plunder, false pretences, vile example, little service and much law' (Bk 3, p. 297). Lady Dedlock's flight and death cause Sir Leicester to suffer a stroke that leaves him for a time speechless and paralysed, and finally 'invalided, bent, and almost blind', watched over by a male nurse, George.

The Dombey and Bounderby empires, the social structure under-pinned by Sir Leicester's prestige and pride, all disintegrate. The causal connection between these events and the unravelling of part of the mystery attaching to the three women is not clear but it is strongly demonstrated. The one obvious link is the effect of the 'reversal' on the three men, which in each case turns out to be physical as well as psychological. In Jewsbury's and Craik's novels it is the women who, in the way traditional for fallen women, pay the price for their (impulse to) transgression: Alice Bryant and Katherine Ogilvie die, Zoe suffers the same penalty vicariously through the sudden loss of her pious husband, whom she has now come to value. In Dickens' narratives, on the contrary, it is the men whose place in society is lost in what seems like a form of retribution for them but which is yet pleasurable to the narrator. It is not that power is now in the hands of the transgressing women but that as bearers of some unseen force they become catalysts for a disaster that manifests itself as exciting. As the narrator says of Louisa in the 'bad seed' passage: 'All closely imprisoned forces rend and destroy. The air that would be healthful to the earth, the water that would enrich it, the heat that would ripen it, tear it when caged up' (*Hard Times*, Bk 3, p. 224). It is this force which erupts and shatters the male-oriented worlds around them: they are revealed as sexual and therefore powerful.

The usual Dickensian narrative pattern, in which accumulated disorder rights itself, is here only faintly evident: disorder and destruction cease, Edith and Louisa return to male tutelage, and no further explosions are predicted. But the more evident pattern is the apparent inevitability of the passionate women's secret sexuality bringing chaos, even though it gradually subsides. What is remarkable here is that the chaos is seen as exciting and desirable, like the women themselves. The texts become charged with the tension resulting from a clash between the conventional language for the representation of women and Dickens' own idiolect. What emerges is not merely an assertion of women's sexual nature but a celebration of its illicit expression. A higher value is ultimately set on passionate women than on nubile girls.

Chapter 6

True mothers

All four signs discussed so far (*nubile girls, fallen girls, excessive females* and *passionate women*) involve an evaluation of the women concerned: they categorise them and simultaneously answer the question 'What is the worth of this kind of woman?' As I have shown, the claim that Dickens rated nubile girls as 'naturally' perfect is contradicted by his explicit assertion that the unrestrained femaleness of excessive females is ludicrous, damaging and hateful. It is true, on the other hand, as is often asserted, that asexuality seems to be a requirement for the nubile girls' perfection, but it is problematised by the ghost-pornography of narratives involving them. Similarly, the conventional condemnation of sexual knowledge in fallen girls is compromised by the magnetic attraction and power attaching to 'passionate' experienced women, which is seen as intensely desirable. In these ways Dickens diversifies the significance of the conventional stereotypes of women already available in narrative language.

Tanner (1979) theorises the adulteresses' potential for creating trouble by explaining why they are so significant to nineteenth-century society in the first place. He points to the fact that marriage, as many have recognised, is the central subject for 'bourgeois novels' because it serves as a paradigm for

> the resolution of problems of bringing unity out of difference, harmony out of opposition, identity out of separation, concord out of discord . . . a means by which society attempts to bring into harmonious alignment patterns of passion and patterns of property . . . it is the structure

that maintains the Structure . . . (. . . all the models, conscious and unconscious, by which society structures all its operations and transactions . . .). (p. 15)

As he sees it, a middle-class woman who marries serves crucially to interrelate several societal functions:

> The figure of the wife ideally contains the biological *female*, the obedient *daughter* (and perhaps sister), the faithful *mate*, the responsible *mother*, and the believing *Christian*, and harmonizes all the patterns that bestow upon her these differing identities. (p. 17)

To commit adultery is to destroy this integrated figure with its crucial power of binding together:

> *Adulteress* points to an activity not an identity; an unfaithful wife, and usually by implication a bad mother, is an unassimilable conflation of what society insists should be separate categories and functions. The wife and mother in one set of social circumstances, should not, and cannot be, [*sic*] the mistress and lover in another. (p. 12)

In this account the adulteress offers a unique narrative potential for generating plots which threaten the whole fabric of bourgeois society by confusing and adulterating social identities.

So the destruction brought about by Dickens' putative adulteresses is not surprising, though the narrators' prurient delight in it may be. As Tanner points out, it is their destructive potential which necessitates the extrusion and devaluing of such women by nineteenth-century society. What will be demonstrated in this chapter is that in Dickens' narratives an even more potent force for disorder is to be found paradoxically in the very women represented as the social ideal. They are more radically destructive than adulteresses; the turbulence they create accounts for the unease within his texts which gives his narratives such ambiguous power. The mechanics of this process can best be understood by a consideration of Dickens' overall structuring of the semantic field relating to women: by examining, as I proposed in chapter 1, the nature of the larger group to which all his positively valued women belong, and from which his disvalued women are excluded. This necessitates identifying the essential qualities which distinguish each of the two groups. It is a process parallel to identifying in colour terms the qualities that cause us to distinguish *crimson, scarlet* and *vermilion* as *red* and *emerald, olive* and *sage* as *green*.

Consequently, the questions now to be asked are: What unifies the disparate groups of women positively valued by Dickens and differentiates them from the disvalued? What distinguishes the womanly from the female? The answer to these questions not only reveals the larger (inclusive) term in this part of the semantic field of gender, but also explains the further disturbance of familial categories already referred to. The questions are ones that Ellis overtly confronts in relation to archetypal 'woman', asking: 'for what is she most valued, admired, and beloved?' (1839:63). As demonstrated in chapter 4, femaleness itself, biologically grounded, depended for Dickens and others on an excess of intuitive faculties over rational ones. What for Ellis and Dickens (as well as Ruskin and the rest) provided the necessary constraint on this excess was an enabling faculty that magically transformed a volatile intuitive responsiveness into a capacity to nurture and cherish. Ellis, answering her own question about what woman is valued for, makes clear the nature of this faculty in her description of its heroic apotheosis:

> For her disinterested kindness. Look at all the heroines whether of romance or reality . . . at all the female characters that are held up for universal admiration. . . . Have these been the learned, the accomplished women; the women who could speak many languages, who could solve problems, and elucidate systems of philosophy? No: or if they have, they have also been women who were dignified with the majesty of moral greatness . . . who, endued with an almost superhuman energy, could trample under-foot every impediment that intervened between them and the accomplishment of some great object . . . while that object was wholly unconnected with their own personal exaltation or enjoyment, and related only to some beloved object, whose suffering was their sorrow, whose good their gain. (Ellis 1839: 63–4)

It is circumstantial demands, therefore, that define the shape of a 'true' woman's nature; and it is upon her plasticity that her value depends – her capacity to be moulded by the shapes of those around her. Characteristically, this process is not described taking place in Dickens' narratives in the heroic arena that Ellis referred to. Demands and pressures for him are the domestic ones provided by the family, which becomes an instrument for extracting more and more 'disinterested kindness' from a person who might otherwise turn into an excessive female. For the latter, of course, as self-directed, does not belong to the larger grouping I am describing.

For Ellis, disinterested kindness, described in terms enforcing an equation with the Christian term *charity*, unfolds into a universal explanation of womanly merit. It explains equally why true women do not need to read Virgil without a dictionary for their own satisfaction, and why 'domestic management' offers a dazzling opportunity to 'evince a high degree of tenderness and affection, . . . which may sometimes be conveyed through this channel when no other is open' (Ellis 1843a: 244–5). For Dickens this satisfaction of demands, motivated by disinterested kindness, is essential to womanly, as opposed to female, identity. From it arise the desirable other-directed qualities of compassion, tenderness, long-sufferingness and self-abnegation. The degree to which intuitive sensibility and a disinterested direction of it are present is the measure of the value that individuals included in this larger grouping possess. Whether Dickens thinks it originates in nature or nurture is hazy, though there is some implication that it is, paradoxically, both natural and cultivated.

Ellis lays much stress on the practical outcome of the magical combination of prized qualities; the emphasis in Dickens is somewhat different. For him the essential form of virtue and value is what Ellis calls 'heart' 'exhibited in modes of deference and acts of consideration as various as the different characters whose good or whose happiness are the subjects of [women's] care' (Ellis 1839: 109). It is evident in Dickens' narratives that the provision of food and physical care are merely sacramental signs of women offering psychological and emotional nurture: 'heart'. It is women themselves who are the most necessary food and the most delicious, as was pointed out in chapter 2. Amy Dorrit can provide only minimally for her father, but is better able to cherish him when presiding over his frugal supper in prison than when he is rich:

> She filled his glass, put all the little matters on the table ready to his hand, and then sat beside him while he ate his supper. Evidently in observance of their nightly custom, she put some bread before herself, and touched his glass with her lips. (*Little Dorrit*, p. 79)

The language of ritual communion reinforces the religious associations of this silent cherishing and evidences the miraculous power of disinterestedness to transform the horrors of rampant femaleness.

It is a quality found, as could be expected, in varying degrees in nubile girls, but also, more surprisingly, in both fallen girls and passionate women. In *David Copperfield* Emily's share of it takes the belated form of the clinging affection Mr Peggotty has so long desired; Martha's of answering his need for an agent to search for the fallen girl and save her from prostitution. Nancy in *Oliver Twist* (who has only her familiar domestic name) cherishes and serves both Sikes and Oliver. And the colour of womanliness, though it appears only in streaks, is more heavily shaded in Nancy and Martha than in some nubile girls. With Nancy it is characterised as a return to 'something of the woman's original nature'. The degree of effort exerted for others by fallen girls even compensates to an extent for their fallen state, which, by contrast, serves to enhance it.

The same is true of passionate women who are not included in the category of the self-directed female described in chapter 4, who 'may not improperly be regarded as a monster' (Ellis 1839: 73). Edith Dombey passionately wishes to cherish and protect the vulnerable Florence; Lady Dedlock is divided by her concern for her illegitimate daughter and for her trusting husband. With them the relationship to an assumed norm of perfection is different from that of fallen girls: their desire to cherish is frustrated by circumstance. Latently only, they are powerful cherishers. In this way the overriding criterion of other-concern (superimposed on sensibility) provides a system of graded value for these three types of women.

To describe the group which includes all those who achieve some success and so some womanly value in this way, the term *true mothers* will be used. The phrase stresses the importance of the capacity to 'mother' or nurture; but typically in Dickens this is not found in those who have actually given birth and who have the societal status of mother. Such women are excluded as monsters of selfishness, unless death made them defect from duty.

If it is accepted that *true mothers* is a suitable description of the superordinate term in Dickens' language of gender, it can be seen to manifest the fact that the whole organisation of the signs relating to women serves the purpose of disvaluing biological mothers. The main method of dismantling them has already been described in chapter 4: they give no hostages to fortune, whereas the necessary condition of true motherhood is the acceptance of responsibility for the welfare of dependants. Excessive females fail to do this, preferring self-nurture in various forms, ranging from Mrs Varden's self-centred histrionics to Mrs Clennam's oysters and partridges. But further reductions in the value of the mother are also brought about by the fact that womanly non-mothers are all potential 'true' mothers.

Such a diminution in the status of those who give birth is particularly pointed when this involves a role reversal between child and defective mother. It happens belatedly in *Dombey and Son* when the embittered Edith responds to her dying mother's craving to be thought the true mother she has never been with motherly forgiveness and solicitude. The episode is virtually repeated, with the issue of motherhood similarly foregrounded, when Edith's *alter ego*, Alice Marwood, on her deathbed, entrusts her cringing procuress mother, like a child, to the care of the virtuous Harriet Carker. Esther Summerson's acceptance of her mother Lady Dedlock's final separation from her has the same force of unconditional parental love:

> I told her . . . that if it were for me, her child . . . to take upon me to forgive her, I did it . . . that my heart overflowed with love for her; that it was natural love, which nothing in the past had changed, or could change. . . . That it was not for me to take her to account . . . but that my duty was to bless her and receive her. (*Bleak House*, p. 510)

The denial that wives who are mothers possess the essential capacity to cherish is made more emphatic by its occurrence in the very category conventionally regarded as their polar opposites: 'old maids'. They had slipped out of Ellis' text altogether because of her preoccupation with the glories of motherhood, which left her no time to discuss them. Yet the defection by death of the infant Paul Dombey's mother is supplied by Miss Tox, a stereotypical spinster, 'wearing such a faded air that she seemed not to have been made in what linen-drapers call "fast colours" originally' (p. 6). This inferior haberdasher's commodity, however, provides the edible Polly Toodle as wet-nurse for the ailing Paul, and watches over him with a maternal care until he is sent away to school. Though she has ambitions to become the second Mrs Dombey, there is no suggestion that her solicitude is pretence. This is made clear by her futile but persistent efforts later to make something of the Toodles' delinquent son, Rob the Grinder. That model of spinsterish eccentricity, 'the little mad old woman', Miss Flite, in *Bleak House* plays the same role in defining Mrs Jellyby's non-motherhood, by remedying her maternal negligence in respect of Caddy's domestic training, so satisfying the girl's craving to make herself into a good wife–housekeeper to young Turveydrop.

The legal status of wife and mother, then, is seen as a disqualification for 'true' motherhood; and the same point is made about the physical act of producing offspring. The pre-pubertal Nell Trent and Amy Dorrit are not even physically capable of maternity when they reveal the mothering power of which they are the supreme exponents, yet they achieve top grading in the assessment of woman. With them may also be grouped Fanny Cleaver (Jenny Wren) in *Our Mutual Friend*. Like the reversal of the mother–daughter role, their physical state denies the significance of biological motherhood. Its concomitant slightness and frailty even serve, by contrast, to heighten the assertion of their powerful other-directedness. It is Nell in *The Old Curiosity Shop*, for instance, who protectively suggests flight to her gambling-addict grandfather, who leads him by the hand, finds him food and water. It is on her shoulder that he sleeps like a child (p. 117); and it is she who wonders what will become of him if she falls ill. These events symbolise their whole relationship, which is characterised by her when she calls him her 'sacred charge', a phrase then used to refer to the Christian duty of mothers in relation to their children. The constant and self-denying performance of 'motherly' service by Nell equates with her high value as a woman, though that adjective is never used in relation to her. None the less, what Dickens is doing by his treatment of her and other 'true' mother figures is shifting the semantic significance of the terms *mother* and *motherhood* away from those to whom it would conventionally attach.

Hence the significance of the fact that the child 'Jenny Wren' takes these terms to herself when faced with a father addicted to alcohol, by referring to him habitually as her 'bad child'. It is by assuming maternal authority that she is able to control him, making him turn out his pockets in order to keep the remnants of his wages for food, and sending him to bed to prevent him from more drinking. Her rebukes to him are always within the same linguistic framework of motherhood: 'A muddling and a swipey old child . . . fit for nothing but to be preserved in the liquor that destroys him . . . if he has no consideration for his liver, has he none for his mother?' (*Our Mutual Friend*, p. 533). After his wretched death she continues to write herself in as his mother by assessing her own culpability for what happened to him:

> 'I felt my responsibility as a mother so much. I tried reasoning, and reasoning failed. I tried coaxing, and coaxing failed. I tried scolding, and scolding failed. But I was bound to try everything, you know, with such a charge upon my hands. Where would have been my duty to my poor lost boy, if I had not tried everything?' (p. 732)

The mechanics of evaluating women in Dickens are made plain here: the worse the child, the more highly regarded the mother who cherishes him; and the more highly regarded the surrogate mother who voluntarily acquires and nurtures dependants, the more disvalued the legal and biological mother who refuses to nurture even non-delinquent offspring. So it can be seen that the overall grouping of womanly figures into a sign, *true mothers*, creates a method of evaluation and at the same time displaces biological mothers from their central place in the family.

It is the repercussions of this displacement that are so powerfully disruptive of familial ties. 'Motherhood' in Dickens' language has become mobile: it can attach to any female, unmarried, young, old or even pre-pubertal. This involves the disturbance of family relationships, which are overwritten by new and more highly valued bonds. Such disruption is in practice far more widespread in Dickens' novels than that caused by the three putative adulteries discussed in chapter 5, though it is of a similar nature. The instances already dealt with involve the overwriting of the roles of mother and daughter, grandfather and female grandchild, father and daughter. Though some of these pairs exist in isolation, others in the same family are often affected. Familial identities merge into each other confusingly and, as will be shown later, sometimes alarmingly. The stable patterns of kinship conventionally assumed to exist begin to dissolve.

In the mid-nineteenth century, of course, orthodox family ties did not carry the same expectations as to what constituted the proper kinds of emotional attachment as in the twentieth century: more emotional intensity between fathers and daughters or between brothers and sisters was, as Davidoff and Hall (1987), amongst others, have pointed out, generally accepted. Also the frequency of maternal death in or after childbirth often led to a daughter or a wife's sister taking over the chief domestic role in the household. Strong bonds then grew up between the widower and the housekeeper. But the incest taboo remained firm, as is clear from, say, the persistence of the legal prohibition against marriage with a deceased wife's sister until 1907.

However, the frequent episodes in which Dickens 'unmothers' families by death or maternal deficiency cannot be directly related to referents in the real world. They must be considered in relation to novelistic language. In this language the displacement of the biological mother appears most strikingly when she is replaced by a daughter, thereby creating a new relationship between father and child. This is consequent on the fact that when Dickens makes such relationships central in his narratives they overwrite the conventional courtship and marriage plot where girls and their suitors are the main concern. The unmothering of a family as an initiating event in *Dombey and Son* and *Little Dorrit,* and the mysterious absence of a mother in *Bleak House* put father and daughter or guardian/father and ward/ daughter into the place conventionally filled by girl and lover. These new relationships are then explored in various ways; but each brings the asexual nubile girl into an ambiguous position reminiscent of the ghost-pornography referred to in chapter 1.

An interesting treatment occurs in *Dombey and Son* where the first Mrs Dombey by weak-mindedly dying at the opening of the novel precipitates her young daughter, Florence, into the role of mother to her infant brother, Paul. It is a place Florence would accept as readily as the thirteen-year-old Charlotte Neckett in *Bleak House.* But in this middle-class world she who is mother is also wife; and the subsequent account of Dombey's displacement and rejection of Florence is fed by that underlying assumption. She is prevented from mothering Paul, and when Dombey marries Edith Granger, her sense of loss and betrayal is profound:

> She dreamed of seeking her father in wildernesses, of following his track up fearful heights, and down into deep mines and caverns; of being charged with something that would release him from extra-ordinary suffering. . . . Then she saw him dead, upon that very bed, and in that very room, and knew that he had never loved her to the last, and fell upon his cold breast, passionately weeping. (*Dombey and Son*, p. 487)

Florence as betrayed wife merges for Dombey with Edith as betraying wife, and after the Edith–Carker elopement she stands in as her stepmother's surrogate to receive Dombey's anger:

> Yielding, at once, to the impulse of her affection. . . . She hastened towards him unchecked, with her arms stretched out . . . as if she would have clasped him round the neck.
>
> And so she would have done. But in his frenzy, he lifted up his cruel arm and struck her, crosswise, with that heaviness, that she tottered on the marble floor; and as he dealt the blow, he told her what Edith was, and bade her follow her, since they had always been in league. (*Dombey and Son*, p. 637)

The pictorial effect here is an icon of the deceived husband's epiphany, often seen in Victorian paintings; but Florence can be represented as an adulteress only if first seen as a wife.

It is noticeable also how the device of tyrannically jealous anger or drunkenness directed towards a woman reinforces her wifely role. It was the kind of situation on which Ellis gave advice to wives, stressing the opportunity offered for yet more service and self-abnegation. Sufferers of this sort who, like Florence, become more perfectly the mother–wife are both Jenny Wren and Lizzie Hexam. With Lizzie the pattern of violence develops further after her father, angered by her sending his son, Charley, to school, appears to threaten her with a knife: 'But, she stopped him with a cry. Looking at her he saw her, with a face quite strange to him, shrinking back against the wall, with her hands before her eyes.' (*Our Mutual Friend*, p. 76). The emotion this posture induces in him suddenly changes the colouring of the scene as Hexam tosses away the knife, asking, 'Can you think I would strike at you with a knife?' and Lizzie drops fainting at his feet:

> He had never seen her so before. He raised her with the utmost tenderness, calling her the best of daughters, and 'my poor pretty creetur,' and laid her head upon his knee, and tried to restore her. But failing, he laid her head gently down again, got a pillow and placed it under her dark hair, and sought on the table for a spoonful of brandy.
> (*Our Mutual Friend*, p. 76)

Hexam's sudden tenderness serves only to heighten the impression that, as in the scenes between Sikes and Nancy, violence is a trope for sexual passion. Lizzie addresses him as 'father', but the substance of this scene lends an uneasy significance to her use of this name.

Florence Dombey and Lizzie Hexam are the central female figures in the texts they inhabit, paradigmatic nubile girls threatened by men, as Kate Nickleby and Nell Trent are in the minor plots of *Nicholas Nickleby* and *The Old Curiosity Shop*; but in each case threatened more violently. But, though Florence and Lizzie are the most prominent and most valued females in the novels involving them, they are, like other nubile girls, marginalised. Amy Dorrit, however, can claim centrality in the whole narrative of the Dorrit family to an extent that makes her unique in Dickens' work: she is the apotheosis of all those girls who reach 'wifehood' via surrogate motherhood. This unexpected focal position is compensated for by a willed invisibility so effective that her presence in Mrs Clennam's room is only retrospectively revealed by Arthur Clennam's question to Affery Flintwich: 'It was a girl, surely, whom I saw near you – almost hidden in the dark corner?' (*Little Dorrit*, p. 39). She has been compared to Shakespeare's Cordelia in what is seen as her magnificently long-suffering silence; but Cordelia's refusal to express more in public than dutiful affection for her father is an act of self-assertion, Amy Dorrit's speechlessness is the perfection of self-abnegation. It is her womanly invisibility and silence which allow Dickens to make her the 'heroine' of the novel, in whom all the desired characteristics of women can be foregrounded and eulogised.

And indeed her surrogate motherhood begins at the preternaturally early age of eight and combines later with the most extreme expression of the idea of nubile girls as edible to produce a central trope pointed out by Sadoff (1982: 56):

> There was a classical daughter once – perhaps – who ministered to her father in his prison as her mother had ministered to her. Little Dorrit, though of the unheroic modern stock, and mere English, did much more, in comforting her father's wasted heart upon her innocent breast, and turning to it a fountain of love and fidelity that never ran dry or waned, through all his years of famine. (*Little Dorrit*, p. 222)

What Sadoff sees in the image of a girl suckling her father is an innocently incestuous sexual relationship. Fatherhood and origins are her main concern and she regards daughters in Dickens as redemptive:

> When I use the term 'incestuous' with regard to Dickens' fathers and daughters, I mean they create a community built on familial structures of desire yet also purified of desire and perfected through idealized love. The figure of the daughter draws to herself the father and lover – the father as lover, the lover as father – and also redeems the desire that calls this incestuous structure into being. (Sadoff 1982: 55)

But on my reading, the incestuous implications are not purified into redemptiveness in the text. There the shock of a female suckling an adult male is increased by the language always used to present Amy Dorrit as little (slight/of asexual appearance): 'a woman, probably of not less than two-and-twenty, she might have been passed in the street for little more than half that age' (p. 52). This early description has been kept constantly in mind by the nickname attached to her surname and pinned to the masthead of the novel as its title. The insistence on a pre-pubertal appearance in women of high value, the attachment of motherhood to the idea of value itself, the definition of motherhood as a capacity to 'give' (in the senses both of 'handing over' and of 'yielding') combine, in what is offered as the perfection of the ideal, into the grotesque image of a person half-woman and half-child, suckling her own father and becoming simultaneously his mother and his wife.

Apart from this biological and sexual abnormality the ideal is further debilitated morally. This is because Amy Dorrit, the ultimate giver, for whom all she does relates only to the object of her affection, behaves in a way strikingly at odds with the conventional moral stance of the narrator; yet he continues to admire the nurturing and to overlook its moral implications. In becoming William Dorrit's mother she takes on other dependants in the shape of her uncle, sister and brother. To the latter in particular she becomes a 'small second mother' who finds him a long series of jobs to lose, and even a chance of emigration, until his insistence on pursuing the road to ruin leads him back to the debtors' prison in his own right. It soon appears that the main service she has to perform for her father is the womanly one of keeping silence: of concealing, in fact, the truth not only about the profligate Tip but about the other more respectable members of the family. Their industry must be kept from him as if it too were a cause of shame:

> With the same hand that had pocketed a collegian's half-crown half an hour ago, he would wipe away the tears that streamed over his cheeks if any reference were made to his daughters' earning their bread. So, over and above her other daily cares, the Child of the Marshalsea had always upon her, the care of preserving the genteel fiction that they were all idle beggars together. (*Little Dorrit*, p. 72)

To maintain this fiction Amy conceals her own work as a seam-stress, her sister Fanny's as a dancer, as well as the fact that the brother whom William Dorrit absent-mindedly ruined, has been driven to earn his living in a theatre orchestra. In practice, her ability to 'suckle', nurture and sustain her father depends on a dedication to deceiving him and to manipulating others also into colluding with his persistent refusal to face reality. These others include her admirer and eventual husband, Arthur Clennam, to whom in Sadoff's account the incestuous father–daughter relationship is transferred and so redeemed. But it is only after William Dorrit's death that a less than rapturous wedding takes place. Meantime Arthur is drawn like others into her elaborate web of deceit. Amy's skill in weaving it depends paradoxically on the magic combination that transforms a female into a creature of womanly virtue: the acutest possible sensibility to her father's neurotic needs and compulsions and a matchless level of that versatility in adapting herself and others to satisfy them of which Ellis speaks so highly (1843b: 322). Amy, offered by the narrator as an instance of the womanly ideal exquisitely achieved, is shown by him as simultaneously perfect and corrupt, as the contradictions and distortions that underlie the conventional representations of gender surface in Dickens' language.

There is one moment at which the text itself registers a strange awareness of this duality when a prostitute, who has taken Amy for a child out at night and the overgrown and retarded woman Maggie for her nurse, realises her mistake as she steps across to kiss Amy and chafe her cold hands: '"Why, my God!" she said, recoiling, "you're a woman!"' (p. 170). The horrified reaction to a child-like woman is negated (dissociated from) by being put into the mouth of a prostitute. But the gratuitousness of the episode (which has no bearing on any other event in the novel) and the complexity of levels of moral judgement involved force a reading of the passage as emphatic: a child–woman, a Little (not Amy) Dorrit is a manifest horror.

Little Dorrit's acute sensibility is the source of a further sense of taint since her wifely role appears to impinge on her consciousness in a way not found with Florence Dombey or Lizzie Hexam. Moreover, it does so in a sexual context in three episodes in the narrative where alternative sexual partners for either her or her father are at issue. In the first she is mildly harassed by the attentions of John Chivery, son of the keeper of the Marshalsea Lock, who has become infatuated with her. She regards her father's slight encouragement of him (in the hope of financial gain) as little less than a form of pimping. Her shocked 'O dear, dear father, how can you, can you, do it!' (p. 211) is more suited to a wife than an unmarried daughter, for though Chivery is of the wrong social class, he is comically honourable in his intentions and conduct. Similarly, it is as though he were William Dorrit that she responds to Arthur Clennam when he plants a lover's kiss on her lips, after telling her that her father is to be released and made rich: 'As he kissed her, she turned her head towards his shoulder, and raised her arm towards his neck; cried out "Father! Father! Father!" and swooned away' (*Little Dorrit*, p. 403).

This is for Sadoff the beginning of the redemptive transference; but a later episode still makes it significantly plain that Amy will brook no other woman as a rival for her father's affections. It happens when William Dorrit himself becomes infatuated with his daughter's companion, Mrs General, and wishes to marry her. Fanny Sparkler (née Dorrit) is against the match from the start on practical financial grounds, but her sister Amy refuses to see what is going on until she feels herself to have cause for jealousy because her father suggests that she herself might marry:

> 'Amy . . . your dear sister . . . has contracted – ha hum – a marriage, eminently calculated to extend the basis of our – ha – connection, and to – hum – consolidate our social relations. My love, I trust that the time is not far distant when some – ha – eligible partner may be found for you . . . it is now a cherished wish and purpose of mine to see you – ha – eligibly (I repeat eligibly) married.' (*Little Dorrit*, p. 590)

Her expression of repugnance, 'O no. . . . Pray!', is characteristically minimal but its motive is not, like Fanny's, a dislike and distrust of Mrs General. It is rather a jealous sense of betrayal which the narrator casts, like the reference to 'the classical daughter', in a subjunctive or hypothetical mood, appropriate in this language to the extremity of her feeling:

> If the thought ever entered Little Dorrit's head . . . that he could give her up lightly now, in his prosperity, and when he had it in his mind to replace her with a second wife, she drove it away. Faithful to him still. (p. 591)

There is a literal truth in the idea that Mrs General would be William Dorrit's second wife, succeeding Amy's dead mother; but the girl's own phrase, 'replace her', referring to herself, makes *her* the faithful wife who is to be displaced. Her insistence on driving out the idea of another wife indicates a picture too horrible to entertain of herself betrayed, supplanted, in effect divorced. Ironically, as a consequence of privileging true (or surrogate) motherhood Dickens presents as the supreme example of womanliness not only a woman who will scheme relentlessly to protect her father's fantasies but who behaves on occasion like a jealous wife.

The revelatory force of the depiction of Amy Dorrit results from two things: the extreme she represents in termms of the Dickensian stereotype of nubile girls and the disruptive effect of making true mothers the category into which all positively-valued women are subsumed. The father–daughter relationships so far indicated as highly valued and yet incestuously coloured are few in number, but their subversiveness is recurrently strengthened when ghost or shadow fathers marry their daughters. Two minor examples are found in *David Copperfield* and in *The Old Curiosity Shop*. Copperfield himself, a highly valued male with no fewer than three surrogate mothers (Miss Peggotty, Aunt Betsy Trotwood and Agnes Wickfield) to serve his needs and enhance his patriarchal status, is an instance. His paternalistic delight in Dora's virginal childishness leaves him after his marriage to her, as an adult who realises too late that he has vexingly married a child under the age of reason if not of consent. Though he succeeds in impregnating her, he reverts to a paternal role in a somewhat martyred fashion. Significantly in a novel of such familial and sexual confusion, this does not prevent him later from marrying one of his surrogate mothers, his 'sister' by annexation, Agnes. Less noticeably, in *The Old Curiosity Shop* Dick Swiveller first rescues a child–drudge, putative daughter of Quilp and Sally Brass, from the latter's clutches; christens her 'The Marchioness'; renames her Sophronia Sphynx before sending her to school; and marries her when she reappears as a suitably nubile daughter.

But the major and most prominent example of this sequence of events occurs in *Bleak House*. When Jarndyce adopts Ada Summerson as a child and later brings her to Bleak House, he puts himself *in loco parentis* by becoming her guardian as much as Ada Clare's or Richard Carstone's. However, she is singled out for an ambiguous servant status, which delights him, as that of Hannah Cullwick delighted the middle-class A.J. Munby, who perpetuated it via a lengthy *folie à deux*. Eventually, at the age of sixty, he asks his little housekeeping Esther to marry him, though she is by now about a third of his age. His 'reminder' that she owes him nothing is readily translated by Esther – she owes him everything: 'To devote my life to his happiness was to thank him poorly, and what had I wished for the other night but some new means of thanking him?' (*Bleak House*, p. 611).

The difference between Esther and Hannah Cullwick, who eventually married Munby, is that though she agrees, she is not a willing partner in this bizarre sexual scheme: she is already officially in love with Woodcourt when she acquiesces in Jarndyce's moral blackmail. This fact undermines the narrator's insistence on Jarndyce's act as benign, and further disturbs the cosily domestic values supposed to be represented by the (now doubly ironic) name Bleak

House. Jarndyce's final decision to waive his 'claim' in favour of Woodcourt comes as no more than a belated return to surface propriety after an episode of stark exploitation. The narrator is able to offer no satisfactory explanation of the private grief that her acquiescence inflicts on Esther. The episode demonstrates clearly that the dislocations caused by replacing biological mothers with 'true' ones, and the consequences of that replacement are more disturbing than those evoked by the putative adulteresses: because, amongst other things, they emanate from valued figures.

It is noticeable that *Bleak House*, the site of some of the most intense of these contradictory figures and sequences, generates a paratactic episode on the periphery of the text that can be read as a pointed reference to forbidden sexual relationships. It is written in a ludic language, reminiscent of 'The four sisters' which, as shown in chapter 2, related in the same way to the iterability of nubile girls. In *Bleak House* the joke takes the form of an account of the perfectly legally married pair, Mr and Mrs Bayham Badger, whose identity is constituted not by the very minor role that they play in the plot but by their eccentric verbal resurrections of Mrs Badger's two previous husbands, Captain Swosser and Professor Dingo. These two are, in effect, brought back from the grave by incessant references to their appearance, habits and distinction so that they form a polygamous quartet with the Badgers. The suggestion of multiple bigamy is underlined by Badger's revelation that 'Mrs. Badger has been married to three husbands – two of them highly distinguished men . . . and, each time, upon the twenty-first of March at Eleven in the forenoon!' (*Bleak House*, p. 174). Though these other two husbands of his wife are overtly referred to by Badger as an enhancement of his own status and distinction, the prurient joke underlying his claim is that what they have all three really shared is Mrs Badger's bed, or rather Mrs Badger. Using the form of a joke made paratactically it is once again possible for Dickens to refer to his own concealed suggestions, so subversive of the superficial order that his narrators always prescribe.

As can be seen, the dissolution of conventional kinship patterns involves the development of unorthodox sexual bonds. This disorder is increased by an accompanying subversion of the gender roles that underpin familial identities and are more basic than they. As Poovey (1989), for instance, puts it 'The epistemological term *woman* could guarantee men's identity only if difference was fixed' (p. 80): an absolute opposition between male and female was a social necessity for the construction of the family in mid-nineteenth-century terms; and the opposition turns out not to be absolute in Dickens' novels. Though the breakdowns in it are few, they are crucial to the nature of the unease that is a large part of the power of the later narratives. They increasingly contradict the bland patterning of plots that turn surface disorder into order: for they are part of that disorder and yet projected as admirable and desirable.

A mark of this is that they tend to occur by a kind of seepage into the text where a particularly intense relationship, privileged as specifically innocent by the narrator, develops between two people, even if they are of the same gender. Only rarely does this happen through a relationship between two men, though there is an exceptional instance in the case of James Steerforth and David Copperfield. The latter is the (metaphorical) third victim of a practised seducer with two female victims, Rosa Dartle and Little Emily, already to his credit. It is he who makes the parallel clear when he regenders Copperfield with a new name: 'My dear young Davy, . . . you are a very Daisy. The daisy of the field, at sunrise, is not fresher than you are!' (*David Copperfield*, p. 246). This allusion to his girlish naivety sticks, and for Steerforth from then on Copperfield is, like his other conquests, a girl, Daisy.

More commonly, the affective relationship that overrides gender norms and so breaks down difference is between two women. There is evidence, for instance, in such letters as those between Jane Carlyle and Geraldine Jewsbury that, when Dickens wrote, intense ties between women were widely acceptable, and since many were ignorant of or disbelieved in lesbian, or what was called 'Sapphic' love, were regarded without suspicion. But some of his portrayals of such ties use language reminiscent of sentimental love affairs which creates contextual unease. It is again in *Bleak House* that an extreme example is found. The measure of excess in the feeling that Esther shows for Ada is the absence of any similar expression of emotion for Woodcourt, with whom she is supposed to be deeply in love. It is on Ada that she lavishes verbal affection (at odds also with her normal self-suppression), referring to her in terms such as a lover in the kind of conventional romance parodied in Miss Twinkleton's reading in *Edwin Drood* might be supposed to use to a sweetheart: 'my darling', 'my beauty', 'my angel girl'. Ada is her main concern when she catches smallpox: how can she keep Ada from infection? How can she endure their separation? And will Ada still love her when she finds her so disfigured by pock-marks? Much is made of her intense fear of rejection on these strange grounds as she awaits their reunion:

> I did not mean to do it, but I ran up-stairs into my room, and hid myself. . . . There I stood trembling, even when I heard my darling calling as she came up-stairs. . . . She ran in. . . . Ah, my angel girl! the old dear look, all love, all fondness, all affection. Nothing else in it. . . . O how happy I was, down upon the floor, with my sweet beautiful girl down upon the floor too, holding my scarred face to her lovely cheek, bathing it with tears and kisses, rocking me to and fro like a child, calling me by every tender name that she could think of, and pressing me to her faithful heart. (*Bleak House*, p. 517)

The blurring of gender boundaries, of 'difference', here facilitates the fluctuations in social roles as each girl becomes lover, mother and daughter to the other. Under the pressure of emotion, relationships collapse easily into one another in Dickens.

A similar episode occurs in *Edwin Drood*, where it has already been prepared for by the ambivalent description of the Landless twins, Helena and Neville, when they first appear:

> An unusually handsome lithe young fellow, and an unusually handsome lithe girl; much alike; both very dark, and very rich in colour; she, of almost the gypsy type; something untamed about them both; a certain air upon them of hunter and huntress; yet withal a certain air of being the objects of the chase, rather than the followers. (*Edwin Drood*, p. 44)

Helena's dark colouring, her 'untamed' quality, and her 'gypsy' look of the social outsider suggest the illicit aura of the passionate woman. This is enhanced by the hints of a secret shared between brother and sister, whilst paradoxically the insistent verbal parallels between the two figure verbally some kind of gender equivalence. The masculine side of Helena's nature is emphasised by the ferocity she shows in protecting Rosa Bud in the face of John Jasper's advances, which so disturb the more delicate and feminine girl. This protectiveness culminates in a scene very like that between Esther and Ada, as Helena embraces the terrified Rosa:

> The lustrous gipsy-face drooped over the clinging arms and bosom, and the wild black hair fell down protectingly over the childish form. There was a slumbering gleam of fire in the intense dark eyes, though they were then softened with compassion and admiration. Let whomsoever it most concerned, look well to it! (*Edwin Drood*, p. 54)

There is a hermaphroditic quality to Helena here: the strongly protective embrace and the gauntlet melodramatically thrown down by the last sentence imply a male identity not contradicted by the use of any gender-specific pronoun; whereas the long 'wild black hair' suggests a woman and one who is, moreover, specified as sexually accessible. Such unfixings of 'difference' as the three listed here contribute markedly to the anarchic subtexts already described, which are evoked by the narrator with such gusto through highly valued characters.

The dissolution of rigid familial categories and of gender difference has a further predictable consequence: the individual's loss of a clear sense of self. Characters slip, like Copperfield or Esther, from one putative identity to another, in the familiar Dickensian process, as others redefine by renaming them. This practice becomes an explicit issue in *Little Dorrit*, as a focus of resentment for Harriet Beadle, 'Pet' Meagles' maid, after she has run away from her employers. Mr Meagles has already explained her nickname, Tattycoram, as Pet's childish corruption of Hatty combined with the name of Thomas Coram, founder of the orphanage where Harriet was brought up. Miss Wade takes a different view of it when ironically encouraging her to return to the Meagles:

> 'You can have your droll name again, playfully pointing you out and setting you apart. . . . (Your birth, you know; you must not forget your birth.) You can again be shown to this gentleman's daughter, Harriet . . . as a living reminder of her own superiority and her gracious condescension.' (*Little Dorrit*, p. 319)

Theoretically, what Miss Wade offers by her pointed use of 'Harriet' here is the girl's own identity; in practice what she proffers is merely a choice between two personae constructed by others, the Meagles' 'Tattycoram' and a Wade-style one replicating her own. Harriet Beadle is at ease with neither but alternates angrily between the two, uncertain where to find her self.

Similar burdens are placed on Esther Summerson by the cluster of identities forced on her as 'No-one's' daughter: Dame Durden, Dame Trot, Mother Hubbard, Little Woman. The last of these needs no comment and the first three commit her to premature middle age. Her literal uncertainty as to who she is, apart from being her 'mother's shame' triggers a dream early on in the narrative:

> At first I was painfully awake, and vainly tried to lose myself, with my eyes closed, among the scenes of the day. At length, by slow degrees,

they became indistinct and mingled. I began to lose the identity of the sleeper resting on me. Now it was Ada; now, one of my old Reading friends from whom I could not believe I had so recently parted. Now, it was the little mad woman worn out with curtseying and smiling; now, someone in authority at Bleak House. Lastly, it was no one, and I was no one. (*Bleak House*, p. 45)

This not only enacts the uncertainty of Esther's grasp on her own subjectivity but its dependence on the shifting identities of those around her. The dream tropes the way that the familial and sexual confusions described in this chapter strike at the basis of the order that Dickens' novels superficially look for and attain. The destructiveness of (non-)adulteresses acts as a magnet for Dickens' narrators because it has the allure of a power as natural and amazing as that of a germinating seed. The attraction of the slippages surrounding nubile girls is even more forceful. They are sacred figures for the narrator, the objects of eulogy and yet catalysts bringing release from the rigid constraints of the orthodox family, with a resultant freeing of affective emotions. They illustrate how covertly the beginning of shifts in novelistic language take place: with the treatment of non-adulteresses it is under the protecting power of the negative; with the treatment of nubile girls it is under the shield of an apparent continuance of gender stereotypes.

The novels mainly referred to in this chapter explicitly address contemporary forms of social injustice which, despite a rhetoric of indignation, they 'resolve' (or rather fail to resolve), as in *Bleak House* and *Little Dorrit*, on a personal and emotional level. They therefore lend themselves to current theories which prefer to read all literary constructions of gender as merely the medium for the containment of political and economic issues. Sometimes the case is powerfully argued, as by Nancy Armstrong in *Desire and Domestic Fiction* (1987). For her the ultimate purpose of all such fiction, including Dickens', was the winning of the 'middle-class struggle for dominance'. In this struggle, the 'creation' and then representation of what Foucault calls 'sexuality' (based on 'difference') is part of the wider strategy of acquiring the means 'to classify any social group and keep it under observation' (p. 201). She argues that in the hands of Dickens and Gaskell 'domestic fiction carried the process of suppressing political resistance into the domain of popular literature, where it charted new domains of aberrance requiring domestication' (1987: 163). But it is only by keeping Dickens' texts in the middle-distance that his work can be treated as a smooth illustration of this bourgeois ideology. Like all literary works closely examined, his show an individual reworking of the communal language. The politics of class and those of gender are tangled together but, on my reading, it is the latter which predominate in Dickens, providing the semantics rather than merely the grammar of his texts.

Support for this view has already been provided in chapter 4, since only *some* of his excessive females combine a monstrous nature with lower-class status, though Armstrong claims that *all* of them do. This is necessary for her generalisation that 'the monstrous woman . . . [is] one step in a series of displacements that eventually relegated a whole realm of social practices to the status of disruption and deviance requiring containment and discipline' (1987: 166). If Dickens attempted to write in the language that Armstrong describes, then close reading of the novels suggests that he failed: Miss Wade in *Little Dorrit*, Rosa Dartle in *David Copperfield* and Lizzie Hexam and Fanny Cleaver in *Our Mutual Friend* all refute a reading that sees women as a means of containing class issues. These women belong to the wrong class for such containment to work: the first two are fallen and should therefore be 'lower class'; the last two are womanly 'true mothers' and therefore should be middle class.

It seems to be the issue of gender that is more basic for Dickens, though in his idiosyncratic reworking of gender stereotypes he makes some use of the conventional language which associates virtue and refinement with the middle classes and vice and unwomanliness with the lower classes. In doing so, however, as pointed out in chapter 1, he manages to reveal rather than conceal the flaws in this connection. I would further argue that in Dickens' narratives, contradictions are revealed rather than hidden: the stereotypes of women conventionally privileged appear as grotesques or as catalysts for male sexual fantasy; disfavoured stereotypes are rehabilitated. At the same time the dream-like anarchy evoked by these processes provides an exhilarating power which becomes the object of the narrators' desire. It is on the explosive force of the Dickensian language for the representation of women that the characteristically disturbing impact of his narratives depends. On a rhetorical level they constitute as much of a hostile reaction to conventional stereotypes of the Victorian family and women as Florence Nightingale's polemic on the domestic as women's only sphere:

The family? It is too narrow a field for the development of an immortal spirit. . . . The family uses people, *not* for what they are, not for what they are intended to be, but for what it wants them for . . . its own uses. This system dooms some minds to incurable infancy, others to silent misery. (in Stark 1979: 37)

Chapter 7

Postscript:
rewriting experience

The preceding chapters have been based on the argument that the stereotypes for Dickens' women are to be found in the language already in use for representing different kinds of female in nineteenth-century writing. This, of course, also involved the assumption that interpretive criticism should look to the text and not to biography as the site of meaning. From a linguistic point of view this is a truism, since biographical criticism is analogous to confusing the *referent* of a word with its *sense*. None the less, discussion of female characters in Dickens' novels has concentrated, even recently, on relating them to his mother, wife, sisters-in-law, daughter and mistress. His work is seen as an extension of his life in which he either therapeutically worked out/off his feelings or took his revenge. With few other Victorian novelists has this treatment been imposed to the same extent. The theoretical arguments for replacing it were made clear in chapter 1. And even in practical terms such criticism is locked into a tautology. It says, for instance, that Mrs Nickleby is Dickens' mother and Dickens' mother is Mrs Nickleby; or that Lucie Manette is Ellen Ternan and Ellen Ternan is Lucie Manette. There is nowhere for such criticism to go except backwards and forwards between the two propositions. However, there is a facile case to be made for the familiar approach, which, because of its persistence, should perhaps be answered on its own terms. That is what I now propose to do.

Biographical accounts by Dickens' contemporaries lend superficial support to the practice of interpreting the women in the novels from his life. They do this by relying on the fact that, in some literal sense, for Dickens the boundaries between fact and fiction dissolved when he was writing. Two of his children at least bear witness to a curious phenomenon. His daughter Mary/Mamie, nicknamed by him for her sweet, bland flavour, Mild Gloster, tells in a much-quoted passage of watching her father at work:

> suddenly he jumped up, went to the looking-glass, rushed back to his writing table and jotted down a few words; back to the glass again, this time talking to his own reflection, or rather to the simulated expression he saw there, and was trying to catch before drawing it in words, then back again to his writing. After a little he got up again, and stood with his back to the glass, talking softly and rapidly for a long time, then *looking* at his daughter, but certainly never *seeing* her, then once more back to his table, and to steady writing. (Mary Dickens 1885: 42)

His eldest son, Charles/Charley was less adoring. He alone of all the children accompanied his mother when Dickens forced her from the marital home in 1858, within a year of meeting the eighteen-year-old actress, Ellen/Nelly Ternan. Charley tells a story similar to his sister's. It is also much cited since it involves a murdered woman and leaves the biographer exciting scope for filling in the real name of the victim. Is it meant to be his mother, his wife or his mother-in-law? Charley tells how, sitting alone (as he thought), at Gad's Hill round about 1867 he heard

> a noise as if a tremendous row were going on outside, and as if two people were engaged in a violent altercation or quarrel, which threatened serious results to somebody. . . . Presently the noise came again, and yet again, worse than before, until I thought it really necessary to ascertain what was going on. Stepping out of the door . . . I soon discovered the cause of the disturbance. There . . . was my father, striding up and down, gesticulating wildly, and in the character of Mr. Sikes, murdering Nancy with every circumstance of the most aggravated brutality. (C. Dickens, younger 1934: 28)

Other 'evidence', on the face of it more strongly supportive of the biographical approach, is found in Dickens' own allusions to his characters as though they were real people. With Nell Trent in *The Old Curiosity Shop* he speaks of slowly murdering her:

> Nobody will miss her like I shall. It is such a very painful thing to me, that I really cannot express my sorrow. Old wounds bleed afresh when I only think of the way of doing it: what the actual doing it will be, God knows. (*Pilgrim Letters*, 2, 181)

He later wrote in another letter: 'I am, for the time being, nearly dead with work – and grief for the loss of my child' (*Pilgrim Letters*, 2, 184).

The converse of the 'factualising' of fiction is the occasional 'fictional' fantasy about real people. He and his friend Maclise concocted, partly in letters, the comic fantasy that they were 'raving with love for the Queen – with a hopeless passion whose extent no tongue can tell, nor mind of man conceive' (*Pilgrim Letters*, 2, 25). Dickens himself later conducted a more ambiguous 'literary' affair with an American woman, Frances Colden, writing comically of her to her husband as 'the beloved Mrs. Colden' (*Pilgrim Letters*, 3, 183). To the woman herself he wrote a parodic love letter culminating in a (for then) slightly *risqué* verse alluding to her shapely figure and the privilege of lacing her stays (*Pilgrim Letters*, 3, 219–20).

This earnest and playful confounding of fact and fiction is clear but the inference to be drawn from it less so. There are, to begin with, at least two different kinds of evidence here: others' descriptions of Dickens and material written by him. His children's reports merely describe his apparent state of mind during composition, and lead nowhere in relation to what he wrote. It is a different matter with his factualising of fiction (as he grieves over what he is doing to Little Nell) or his fictionalising of half-fact (as with Mrs Colden) or of non-fact (as with Queen Victoria). These instances, viewed superficially, suggest that, as far as women go, Dickens' fiction can be treated as fact. However, more carefully considered, they imply that it is in the medium of language that the distinctions between fact and fiction dissolve. They suggest that the usual view should be reversed and another hypothesis examined: that the accounts he gives of the women related to him are as much literary constructs as the fictional women discussed earlier. The support for this would rest on a demonstration that they too are created by the deployment of his familiar literary techniques.

The general point can be illustrated first from a non-tendentious area. John Forster in his *Life of Charles Dickens* (1872–4) quotes a series of vignettes describing women Dickens had met in Switzerland in 1846. In the following sequence I have alternated them with the 'fictional' descriptions in *Sketches by Boz* (1836):

> The Miss Maldertons were dressed in sky-blue satin trimmed with artificial flowers; and Mrs. M. (who was a little fat woman), in ditto ditto, looked like her eldest daughter multiplied by two. (*Sketches by Boz*, p. 357)

an American lady . . . who looked like what we call in old England 'a reg'lar Bunter' – fluffy face (rouged); considerable development of figure; one groggy eye; blue satin dress made low with short sleeves. . . . Also a daughter; face likewise fluffy; figure likewise developed; and one eye not yet actually groggy but going to be. (Forster, 1873: 2, 264)

Miss Amelia Martin was pale, tallish, thin, and two-and-thirty – what ill-natured people would call plain, and police reports interesting. (*Sketches by Boz*, p. 250)

Sir Joseph, a large baronet . . . with a little, loquacious, flat faced, damaged-featured *old young* wife. (Forster 1873: 2, 242)

The method in all these passages is to include satirical stabs amongst the physical itemising of women (of the kind described in chapter 2 above) to make them by implication equally matters of fact. The metonymic and reductive technique is the same for both the 'real' in the letters to Forster and the 'invented' in *Sketches by Boz*. Or does the distinction between 'real', 'invented' and 'observed' not now collapse if they are similarly constructed?

This prepares the ground for the proposition that his characteristic literary shaping is discernible in the more tendentious case of Dickens' accounts of the women around him. The central instance is his young sister-in-law, Mary Hogarth, a fruitful 'source' in biographical criticism for his nubile girls. Yet most of the material drawn on to illustrate the 'real' Mary, with whom literary creations can be compared, comes from Dickens' own letters. It is already at least epistolary literature. And when approached from a detached point of view the material makes visible the evolution of a literary figure, 'Mary'. The process is evident in the series of letters that he wrote to friends and acquaintances after her sudden death on Sunday, 7 May 1837, just over a year after his marriage to her sister Catherine. The kernel of the series is the first and briefest, written to Edward Chapman on the same day:

We are in deep and severe distress. Miss Hogarth after accompanying Mrs. Dickens and myself to the Theatre last night was suddenly taken severely ill, and despite our best endeavours to save her, expired in my arms at two o'Clock this afternoon. (*Pilgrim Letters*, 1, 256)

In subsequent letters the theatrical detail that she 'expired' in his arms is tried out in alternative forms: 'expired' (once more), 'died' (four times), 'breathed her last' (once). To the third letter of the sequence is added the germ of future eulogy – 'she has been the grace and life of our home and the admired of all for her beauty and excellence.' The phrase 'grace and life of our home' is consolidated by repetition in the fourth letter where it is expanded by the addition 'She has been our constant companion since our marriage.' The latter statement is added to the central core by being repeated in the fifth letter. A fairly clear form is now established for the letter, with the emphasis on Mary's virtues, which are linked to the happy domestic scene of Dickens' household.

After her funeral on 17 May a letter to Thomas Beard elaborates the kernel further. 'She died in my arms' now becomes the rhetorical 'Thank God she died in my arms and' – a new touch – 'the very last words she whispered were of me' (*Pilgrim Letters*, 1, 259). Similarly, the earlier 'grace and life of our home' is expanded into a panegyric that detaches her from Dickens' hearth and from his wife: 'I solemnly believe that so perfect a creature never breathed. I knew her inmost heart, and her real worth and value. She had not a fault.' The new hyperbole and its elegant contrast with the studied simplicity of the last sentence are striking. So too is the male appropriation of her: from being shared with his wife she now becomes his alone. Indeed, Kate is presented in this letter as more resilient in the face of her loss (although in fact it was thought to have brought on her miscarriage). In another letter, written on the same day, he refers to Mary as the person 'whom I loved, *after my wife*, more deeply and fervently than anyone on earth' (*Pilgrim Letters*, 1, 260; my italics). As Slater (1983: 82) points out, this qualification was not made again.

By 31 May 1837 Dickens was writing of Mary at length as 'the dearest friend I ever had'. He once again uses the familiar formulae 'the grace and life of our home', 'our constant companion', but only in passing. The main emphasis falls on the eulogy, which reinforces the strongest of personal claims:

> Words cannot describe the pride I felt in her, and the devoted attachment I bore her. She well deserved it, for with abilities beyond her years, with every attraction of youth and beauty, and conscious as she must have been of everybody's admiration, she had not a single fault. (*Pilgrim Letters*, 1, 263)

By this time there is a firmly established literary exemplar which could be adapted later when Dickens needed to write a *consolatium* for the publisher Bradbury when his young daughter died in 1839. It is a highly stylised piece, built around the argument that the kind of spiritual consolation available to those who have lost 'a young and promising girl' before she could become anything worse, can only be properly understood by those who have suffered a similar affliction. The argument provides the setting for a centrepiece in which he draws a parallel between Bradbury's loss of his daughter and his own loss of Mary:

> It is nearly two years ago since I lost in one short night a young and lovely creature whom – I can say even to *you* now – I loved with the warmest affection that our nature is capable of, and in whom I had the fondest father's pride. The first burst of anguish over, I have never thought of her with pain – never. I have never connected her idea with the grave in which she lies. I look upon it as I sometimes do upon the clothes she used to wear. They will moulder away in their secret places, as her earthly form will in the ground, but I have long since learnt to separate her from all this litter of dust and ashes, and to picture her to myself with every well-remembered grace and beauty heightened by the light of Heaven. (*Pilgrim Letters*, 1, 516)

The rhetoric concludes neatly with the hope that Bradbury will also at a not-too-distant date have the same experience of 'softened regret'.

There are noticeable contradictions here with other statements made in letters about Mary Hogarth: 'I have never thought of her with pain' contradicts remarks elsewhere about old wounds bleeding afresh; his claim never to have connected her with her grave contrasts with his repeatedly expressed desire to be buried in it and grief at the thought of not being. My purpose in drawing attention to these contradictions is to point out that writing a consolatory elegy to a grieving father involves appropriate alteration of the exemplar.

At the same time the exemplar is developing in a characteristically Dickensian way as Mary's identity changes. In the Bradbury letter the new stress on Mary's beauty, taken with the reference to 'the warmest affection that our nature is capable of', turns her into a wife or mistress; simultaneously she is seen as a daughter in whom he had 'the fondest father's pride'. She has acquired the kind of polyvalent identity discussed in chapter 6; and it has developed in the writing and rewriting of her. The reference to her clothes is taken by Slater (1983: 85) as literally true; but he may be wrong to take 'I look upon [her grave] . . . and the clothes she used to wear' as a reference to the physical act of looking. The natural interpretation of 'look upon' etc., however, seems to be 'I think of her grave as I think of the clothes she used to wear': the secret places may be entirely metaphorical. But whether literal or not, the (dead) body–(old) clothes equation is a macabre reworking of the language of women as garments which Dickens makes simpler use of in his description of nubile girls.

The last adaptation of the literary 'Mary' is a metamorphosis into a Beatrice spirit-figure, described in a letter written to Forster from Genoa in 1844, some seven years after her death:

> Let me tell you of a curious dream I had . . . I was visited by a Spirit. . . . It wore a blue drapery, as the Madonna might in a picture by Raphael. . . . I knew it was poor Mary's spirit. I was not at all afraid, but in a great delight, so that I wept very much, and stretching out my arms to it called it 'Dear'. (*Pilgrim Letters*, 4, 196)

The passage is well known for what follows: a stilted dialogue, reported verbatim and ending with a recommendation that for him Roman Catholicism would be the best religion. What is more striking is the move to a pseudo-religious register in the last sentence to match the spiritual status of the woman and the startling allusion that makes Dickens' dead sister-in-law the doubly virgin/Virgin Mary. The pun works as the kind of ludic subversion of his own practice that has been pointed out elsewhere in his work, in such instances as the story of 'The four sisters', cited in chapter 2. In brief, the sequence of letters written after Mary's death allows us to see the literary processes at work: 'Mary Hogarth' is as much a literary construct as Kate Nickleby or Nell Trent.

The same is true of the figure of his wife as represented in the letters he wrote at the time of their separation and after it. She is 'described' at some length in a document dated 25 May 1858 and given to Arthur Smith to be shown where necessary in defence of his conduct. It was published in the *New York Tribune* in August 1858. In it he accused his wife of domestic incompetence and gross inadequacy as a mother. Because of this, he writes, his sister-in-law, Georgina, had to be the children's 'playmate, nurse, instructress, friend, protector, adviser, and companion':

> In the manly consideration toward Mrs. Dickens which I owe to my wife, I will merely remark of her that the peculiarity of her character has thrown all the children on someone else. . . . I cannot by any stretch of fancy imagine – what would have become of them but for this aunt. (*Nonesuch Letters*, 3, 22)

This picture of Catherine's maternal defects is elaborated in a letter also written in May 1858 to Angela Burdett-Coutts, the high-minded rich woman with whom he had helped found Urania Cottage, a home for fallen women:

> If the children loved her, or ever had loved her, this severance would have been a far easier thing than it is. But she has never attached one of them to herself, never played with them in their infancy, never attracted their confidence as they have grown older, never presented herself before them in the aspect of a mother. I have seen them fall off from her in a natural – not *un*natural – progress of estrangement . . . Mary and Katey . . . harden into stone figures of girls when they can be got to go near her, and have their hearts shut up in her presence as if they were closed by some horrid spring. (Johnson 1952: 354–5)

The structural rhetoric of this works to negate and denature Catherine as a mother. The poignant equivalent of an 'if only!' is resoundingly answered by the tolling 'never . . . never . . . never . . . never . . .'. These denials systematically exclude every possible time and every possible way in which she might have behaved as a 'true' mother. The strategy is completed by the images of Mary and Katey frozen to stone and with hearts snapped shut by this gorgon: they serve to block any escape for Catherine from the stasis enacted here.

On several occasions Dickens also characterised his wife as subject to some kind of mental disturbance. In the letter to Burdett-Coutts he speaks vaguely of how Catherine, feeling herself to be 'at the disadvantage of groping blindly about me, and never touching me . . . has fallen into the most miserable weaknesses and jealousy . . . at times, been certainly confused besides' (Johnson 1952: 355–6). The same madwoman out of the attic is alluded to less delicately in the painfully public letter in the *New York Tribune* which tells how 'her always increasing estrangement made a mental disorder under which she sometimes labors – more' (*Nonesuch Letters*, 3, 22).

This highly charged account of 'Catherine Dickens' is set in a verbal picture of an incompatibility dating back to the period before Mary's death. The now canonised Mary, indeed, is said to have witnessed and 'understood' it, and so presumably authenticates the allegations. Consequently, biographers and biographical critics have searched conscientiously for shreds of evidence in early letters to substantiate these later detailed allegations. One of the most scrupulous in sifting the evidence is Slater (1983), who is sceptical of minor references to Catherine's defects before an allusion in 1855 to the 'indescribable lassitude' that she has passed on to their eldest son (Slater 1983: 134). Overall, it appears that there is a marked absence of documentary support from Dickens himself for the picture of his wife and their long-established marital misery that he drew in 1858. This underlines forcibly the way that some women in novels which predate the separation do resemble the picture. The women in question are included amongst those described in chapter 4 as excessive females. For that is evidently how, by 1858, Dickens wished to rewrite his wife: as an unreconstructed hysterical female and not a 'true' mother.

The neglect of her children (for which evidence in earlier letters is lacking and evidence to the contrary is present) is anticipated by the behaviour of Mrs Jellyby in *Bleak House* (1853). The rescue work for the Jellyby children that is provided first by Esther Summerson and then by her pupil, Caddy Jellyby, looks forward to the labours of Georgina as described by Dickens. The references to Catherine's unstable mental condition are vague. The malady is intermittent and evidently not acute enough to have been noticed by the world at large. It is clearly not claimed to be psychotic and hallucinatory, but is rather a form of mental confusion. The impression conveyed by the letter to Burdett-Coutts is that she is disorientated ('groping about') and incoherent ('confused'). This sounds like the illogicality and inconsequentiality that, as shown in chapter 4, mark out excessive females in the unschooled state typified by Mrs Gamp. Catherine's self-absorption and the deadening effect she has on her daughters are reminiscent of the egotism and unwarranted self-pity with which Mrs Varden in *Barnaby Rudge* (1841) spoils the domestic peace of her husband and daughter. Catherine's alleged jealousy and inability to see things in their true light are analogous to the dramatising of Mrs Varden, Mrs Gamp in *Martin Chuzzlewit* (1844) and Mrs Skewton in *Dombey and Son* (1848). Yet these fictional women are assumed by biographical critics to be based on Dickens' mother, Elizabeth, whom he strongly disliked. It can be argued that the incompetent, unmaternal and slightly dotty 'Catherine' who appears in the letters in 1858 (usually as 'my wife' or 'Mrs. Dickens') is a new literary creation concocted from earlier fiction, and not a skeleton long concealed in the cupboard.

Like the 'Mary' figure, this one also shifts as context requires. The major adaptation fits the changing narrative to which the letters allude. In the original plot Catherine is a weakly amiable and occasionally unbalanced woman manipulated by her wicked mother and sister (Helen). As Dickens' need for self-exculpation became or was perceived as more extreme, so too did the nature of the story he told. In its later and more sensational version Catherine has deeply wounded him in some mysteriously unspeakable way. He is too afflicted to be reconciled even when the would-be mediator is Burdett-Coutts, who was still trying as late as 1860 to effect a reunion. This attempt elicited the most sensational account of the Catherine story: 'In the last two years, I have been stabbed too often and too deep not to have a settled knowledge of the wounded place' (Johnson 1952: 369). His rewriting of Catherine in all this treats her as later Angel Clare is to treat Tess Durbeyfield when he says after her confession about the affair with Alec: 'You were one person; now you are another. . . . The woman I have been loving is not you' (ch. 35). In early letters, round about the time of their marriage, Dickens addressed his wife as 'my dearest girl', 'my dearest mouse', 'dearest pig' and for most of their married life as 'my dearest Kate'. Now in the letter to Burdett-Coutts she becomes 'a page in my life which once had writing on it' and now 'has become absolutely blank'. And he continues 'it is not in my power to pretend that it has a solitary word upon it' (Johnson 1952: 376). This says in conventional terms more than that she means nothing to him. As the parallel with Tess shows, it means to the nineteenth-century reader that she is a familiar kind of non-person found in marital disputes: the excessive female of earlier letters has been replaced by a metaphorically fallen woman. The issue of sexual transgression with which all the letters negotiate has finally found a location. Catherine is ambiguously the guilty party, too guilty to have intercourse with. For this 'reason' he never saw her again.

The rewriting of his mistress Ellen Ternan is more difficult to come to grips with as there is so little material, but the shreds that remain are suggestive. In her literary construction negative language is predominant: she is not a fallen woman. This is boldly asserted in the statement that he published in *Household Words* shortly after separation from Catherine:

> By some means, arising out of wickedness, or out of folly, or out of
> inconceivable wild chance . . . this trouble has been made the occasion
> of misrepresentations, most grossly false, most monstrous and most

cruel . . . involving . . . innocent persons of whom I have no knowledge if indeed they have any existence. . . . I most solemnly declare . . . that all the lately whispered rumours . . . are abominably false. (*Household Words*, 12 June 1858, p. 1)

Nelly is so emphatically not fallen that she moves from being not fallen to a state of possible non-existence in which transgression would not be thinkable.

Round about the same time, in the *New York Tribune* piece, a familiarly polyvalent identity is attached to her. In this letter Dickens alludes to 'a young lady for whom I have great attachment and regard'. This might be assumed to refer to his sister-in-law, Georgina, who, by remaining with him when Catherine left, laid herself open to rumours of an incestuous relationship with him. But it serves also as a reference to Ellen/Nelly, and could apply to either woman since, significantly, both are describable in the same terms: 'Upon my soul and honor, there is not on this earth a more virtuous and spotless creature than that young lady. I know her to be innocent and pure, and as good as my own dear daughters' (*Nonesuch Letters*, 3, 23). 'That young lady' is Georgina and Ellen or both and her/their relationship to him is like that of Mamie and Katey. Multiple identity proves a useful device here to neutralise stand-in wife and mistress-to-be into daughter figures. This letter parodies the technique of creating shifting familial identity with characters like Amy Dorrit by using it for purposes of obfuscation.

Much later, in July 1867 (though *Nonesuch* gives a date in 1866), by a similar kind of Dickensian magic writing, Ellen is finally translated into someone who in a strange subliminal way is a palimpsest of fallen girl overwritten as nubile girl. Dickens was writing to Frances Elliott, wife of the Dean of Bristol, who had asked to be introduced to Nelly. He replied:

I feel your affectionate letter truly and deeply, but it would be inexpressibly painful to N. to think that you knew her history. . . . She would not believe you could see her with my eyes, or know her with my mind. Such a presentation is impossible. It would distress her for the rest of her life. I thank you none the less, but it is quite out of the question. If she could bear that, she could not have the pride and self reliance which (mingled with the gentlest nature) has borne her, alone, through so much. (*Nonesuch Letters*, 3, 475–6)

The breathtaking equivocation here is on a par with the dangerously ludic episodes like the story of 'The four sisters', as described in chapter 2, or the account of the Bayham Badgers in *Bleak House*, referred to in chapter 6. When Nancy, the prostitute, meets the pure Rose Maylie in *Oliver Twist* she is shamed; so too is the other prostitute, Martha Endell, confronting the still stainless Emily in *David Copperfield*. For a fallen woman the encounter with a respectable one elicits shame at the contrast they make. That is why Nelly could not bear to meet a respectable married woman who knew 'her history' as Dickens' secret mistress for several years. They could only read that story as the start of a harlot's progress. Dickens alone is the super reader who can rewrite such a woman to make her a person as self-reliant, proud and (as her reluctance indicates) as morally fastidious as any nubile girl. 'This is and is not Cressid', as Shakespeare's Troilus says at a moment of crucial revelation.

'Nelly', 'N', 'the riddle', the 'magic circle of one', 'the magic' is for the moment both fallen and spotlessly nubile. For the rest of the time, she is, as Tomalin (1990) says, 'the invisible woman' carefully edited out of documents and life. However, in the Elliott letter her representation brings together interestingly, and not altogether surprisingly, given the ghost-pornography referred to in chapter 2 and the ambivalent figures of chapter 6, two kinds of women who conventionally had nothing in common. By fusing them in the figure of 'N', Dickens perhaps creates his most sophisticated literary representation of a woman: one who enacts the ambiguity of his mapping of overtly contrasting groups of women. She suggests that for him the object of desire has to be simultaneously unfallen and fallen.

So it is demonstrable that these sources of Dickens' women, long regarded as extralinguistic, are not: they can be subjected to the same kind of linguistic analysis as preceding chapters have applied to figures in the novels. Treating them in the traditional way results in an impoverished reading of the texts, and fails to do justice to the ambiguity and uneasy power that I have tried to demonstrate. It does not allow for a recognition of the individualistic slippage of novelistic language relating to women that can be seen taking place in Dickens' work.

References

Acton, William (1857) *Prostitution Considered in its Moral, Social and Sanitary Aspects in London and other Large Cities; with Proposals for the Mitigation and Prevention of its Attendant Evil*, John Churchill, London.

Armstrong, Nancy (1987) *Desire and Domestic Fiction: A political history of the novel*, Oxford University Press, Oxford and New York.

Auerbach, Nina (1982) *Women and the Demon: The life of a Victorian myth*, Harvard University Press, Cambridge, Mass.

Bassein, Beth Ann (1984) *Women and Death: Linkages in western thought and literature* (Contributions to Women's Studies 44), Greenwood Press, Westport, Conn., and London.

Beer, Gillian (1983) *Darwin's Plots: Evolutionary narrative in Darwin, George Eliot and nineteenth-century fiction*, Routledge and Kegan Paul, London.

Belsey, Catherine (1980) *Critical Practice*, Methuen, London and New York.

Blackwood's Edinburgh Magazine (1824) 'Men and women; brief hypothesis concerning the difference in their genius', 16 (93), 387–94.

Carey, John (1973) *The Violent Effigy: A study of Dickens' imagination*, Faber and Faber, London.

Collins, Philip (1971) *The Critical Heritage*, Barnes and Noble, New York.

Craik, Dinah Mulock (1846) *The Ogilvies*, Chapman and Hall, London.

Craik, Dinah Mulock (1858) *A Woman's Thoughts About Women*, Hurst and Blackett, London.

Davidoff, Leonore and Catherine Hall (1987) *Family Fortunes: Men and women of the English middle class, 1780–1850*, Hutchinson, London.

Dexter, Walter (1938) *The Letters of Charles Dickens*, Nonesuch Press, London.

Dickens, Charles (1981) *David Copperfield*, ed. Nina Burgis, Clarendon Press, Oxford.

Dickens, Charles (1974) *Dombey and Son*, ed. Alan Horsman, Clarendon Press, Oxford.

145

Dickens, Charles (1979) *Little Dorrit*, ed. Harvey Peter Sucksmith, Clarendon Press, Oxford.

Dickens Charles (1982) *Martin Chuzzlewit*, ed. Margaret Cardwell, Clarendon Press, Oxford.

Dickens, Charles (1972) *The Mystery of Edwin Drood*, ed. Margaret Cardwell, Clarendon Press, Oxford.

Dickens, Charles (1966) *Oliver Twist*, ed. Kathleen Tillotson, Clarendon Press, Oxford.

Dickens, Charles (younger) (1934) 'Personal reminiscences of my father by Charles Dickens, the eldest son of the great novelist', *Supplement to the Christmas Windsor*, Ward, Lock, London.

Dickens, Mary (1885) 'Charles Dickens at home: with especial reference to his relations with children; by his eldest daughter', *Cornhill Magazine*, NS 10 (Jan.), 32–51.

Ellis, Sarah Stickney (1839) *The Women of England, Their Social Duties and Domestic Habits*, Fisher, London.

Ellis, Sarah Stickney (1843a) *The Wives of England: Their Relative Duties, Domestic Influence, and Social Obligations*, Fisher, London.

Ellis, Sarah Stickney (1843b) *The Mothers of England: Their influence and responsibility*, Fisher, London.

Ellis, Sarah Stickney (1845) *The Daughters of England: Their position in society, character, and responsibilities*, Fisher, London.

Fahnestock, Jeanne (1981) 'The heroine of irregular features: physiognomy and conventions of heroine description', *Victorian Studies*, 24 (3), 325–50.

Forster, John (1872–4) *The Life of Charles Dickens 1812–70*, 3 vols, Chapman and Hall, London.

Garrett, Peter K. (1980) *The Victorian Multiplot Novel: Studies in dialogical form*, Yale University Press, New Haven and London.

Gilman, Sander (1985) *Difference and Pathology*, Cornell University Press, Ithaca N.Y.

Greenwood, James (1869) *The Seven Curses of London*, Stanley Rivers, London.

Greg, W.R. (1850) 'Prostitution', *Westminster Review*, 53, 448–506.

House, Madeleine, Kathleen Tillotson, Graham Storey and Kenneth J. Fielding (eds) (1965–88) *The Pilgrim Edition, The Letters of Charles Dickens*, 6 vols, Clarendon Press, Oxford.

Hunt, Leigh (1825) 'Criticism on female beauty', *New Monthly Magazine and Literary Journal*, 14 (1), 70–7.

Ingham, Patricia (1989) *Thomas Hardy: A feminist reading*, Harvester Wheatsheaf, Hemel Hempstead.

Jewsbury, Geraldine (1845) *Zoe*, ed. Shirley Foster, Virago, London, 1989.

Jewsbury, Geraldine (1848) *The Half Sisters*, Chapman and Hall, London.

Johnson, Edgar (1952) *Letters from Charles Dickens to Angela Burdett-Coutts 1841–65*, Jonathan Cape, London.

Kappeler, Susanne (1986) *The Pornography of Representation*, Polity Press, Cambridge.

Mayhew, Henry (1861–2) *London Labour and the London Poor: A cyclopedia of those that will work, those that cannot work, and those that will not work*, Griffin, Bohn, London; rep. Mayhew, New York, 1968.

Michie, Helena (1987) *The Flesh Made Word: Female figures and women's bodies*, Oxford University Press, Oxford and New York.

Miller, James (1859) *Prostitution Considered in Relation to its Cause and Cure*, Sutherland and Knox, Edinburgh; Simpkin, Marshall, London.

✳ Nead, Lynda (1988) *Myths of Sexuality: Representations of women in Victorian Britain*, Blackwell, Oxford.

Nightingale, Florence (1860) *Suggestions for Thought to Searchers after Religious Truth*, Eyre and Spottiswoode, London.

North British Review (1850) 'The social position of woman', 14, 515–40.

Page, Norman (1973) *Speech in the English Novel*, Longman, London.

Poovey, Mary (1989) *Uneven Developments: The ideological work of gender in mid-Victorian England*, Virago, London; first published University of Chicago, 1988.

Ruskin, John (1865) *Sesame and Lilies: Two lectures delivered at Manchester in 1864*, Smith, Elder, London.

Sadoff, Dianne (1982) *Monsters of Affection: Dickens, Eliot and Bronte on fatherhood*, Johns Hopkins University Press, Baltimore and London.

Shorter, Clement (1908) *The Brontes: Life and letters*, Hodder and Stoughton, London.

Slater, Michael (1983) *Dickens and Women*, Dent, London.

Stark, Myra (ed.) (1979) *Cassandra: An essay by Florence Nightingale*, The Feminist Press, City University of New York.

Strachey, James (ed.) (1961) *The Standard Edition of the Complete Psychological Works of Sigmund Freud*, 19, 235–9, Hogarth Press, London.

Tait, William (1840) *Magdalenism: An inquiry into the extent, causes, and consequences of prostitution in Edinburgh*, P. Rickard, Edinburgh.

Tanner, Tony (1979) *Adultery in the Novel: Contract and transgression*, Johns Hopkins University Press, Baltimore and London.

Tomalin, Claire (1990) *The Invisible Woman: The story of Nelly Ternan and Charles Dickens*, Viking, London.

Walker, Alexander (1834) *Physiognomy Founded on Physiology and Applied to Various Countries, Professions and Individuals*, Smith, Elder, London.

Walkowitz, Judith R. (1980) *Prostitution and Victorian Society: Women, class and the state*, Cambridge University Press, Cambridge.

Index